Toby Olson

*Collected Later Poems*

Also by Toby Olson

Poetry
*The Hawk-Foot Poems*, Abraxas Press, Madison, WI, 1969
*Maps*, Perishable Press, Mount Horeb, WI, 1969
*Worms into Nails*, Perishable Press, Mount Horeb, WI, 1969
*The Brand*, Perishable Press, Mount Horeb, WI, 1969
*Pig/s Book*, Doctor Generosity Press, New York, 1969
*Vectors*, Albatross Press & Ziggurat / Membrane Press, Milwaukee, WI, 1972
*Fishing*, Perishable Press, Mt Horeb, WI, 1973
*The Wrestlers, and other poems*, Barlenmir House, New York, 1974
*City*, Membrane Press, Milwaukee, WI, 1974
*Changing Appearance: Poems 1965–70*, Membrane Press, Milwaukee, WI, 1975
*Home*, Membrane Press, Milwaukee, WI, 1976
*Doctor Miriam*, Perishable Press, Mt Horeb, WI, 1977
*Aesthetics*, Membrane Press, Milwaukee, WI, 1978
*The Florence Poems*, Permanent Press, London, 1978
*Still / Quiet*, Landlocked Press, Madison, WI, 1979
*Birdsongs*, Perishable Press. Mt Horeb, WI, 1980
*We Are the Fire*, New Directions, New York, 1984
*Unfinished Building*, Coffee House Press, Minneapolis, MN 1993
*Human Nature*, New Directions, New York, 2000
*Darklight*, Shearsman Books, Exeter, 2007
*Death Sentences*, Shearsman Books, Bristol, 2019
*Collected Earlier Poems*, Shearsman Books, Bristol, 2024

Fiction
*The Life of Jesus: An Apocryphal Novel*, New Directions, New York, 1976; 2nd ed. Green Integer, Los Angeles, 2018
*Seaview*, New Directions, New York, 1982, 2nd ed. Hawthorne Books, Portland, OR, 2006
*The Woman Who Escaped from Shame*, Random House, New York, 1986
*Utah*, Simon & Schuster, New York, NY, 1987; 2nd ed. Green Integer, Los Angeles, 2003
*Dorit in Lesbos*, Simon & Schuster, New York, NY, 1990
*At Sea*, Simon and Schuster, New York, NY, 1993
*Write Letter to Billy*, Coffee House, Minneapolis, MN, 2000
*The Blond Box*, FC2, Normal, IL, 2003
*The Bitter Half*, FC2, Tuscaloosa, AL, 2006
*Tampico*, University of Texas Press, Austin, TX, 2008
*Walking*, Occidental Square Press, Seattle, WA, 2019
*Journey on a Dime*, GrandIota, Hastings & Brighton, 2021 (short stories)

Other
*The Other Woman*, Shearsman Books, Bristol, 2015 (memoir)

# Toby Olson

# Collected Later Poems

Shearsman Books

First published in the United Kingdom in 2024 by
Shearsman Books Ltd
PO Box 4239
Swindon
SN3 9FN

Shearsman Books Ltd Registered Office
30–31 St. James Place, Mangotsfield, Bristol BS16 9JB
*(this address not for correspondence)*

ISBN 978-1-84861-923-4

Copyright © Toby Olson, 1993, 2000, 2007, 2019, 2024

The right of Toby Olson to be identified as the author of this work has been asserted by him in accordance with the Copyrights, Designs and Patents Act of 1988. All rights reserved.

Acknowledgements

The poems collected here previously appeared in the following volumes:

*Unfinished Building*, Coffee House Press, Minneapolis, MN, 1993
*Human Nature*, New Directions, New York, 2000
*Darklight*, Shearsman Books, Exeter, 2007
*Death Sentences*, Shearsman Books, Bristol, 2019

Further acknowledgements may be found at the end of the book.

# Contents

## Unfinished Building

Rose Poem / 13
American Scat / 15
Clouds / 22
Unfinished Building / 32
El Monte / 42
Floobie / 46
Tide Trail / 51
Come Here / 53
Another Popular Song / 59
Alvina / 61
Standard–9, *Just One (Some) of Those Things* / 64
Standard–13, *I Remember Clifford* / 74
Shining Hour / 80
Here's That Rainy Day / 82

## Human Nature

Sled / 99
Spring Is Here / 106
Collaborative Piece / 110
Oppressive Heat / 112
Moose / 114
Facing / 123
Heavenly Weather / 124
My Daughter / 126
My Son / 133
Little Angel / 139
About This / 141
Cloud-Castle Blues / 142
Angry Opening / 151

Old Musical Chair / 152
Standard–15, *My Old Flame* / 153
Just This Again / 161
Remarkable Storm / 162
Wanda and I / 163
Typical Sad Song / 185
The Sign / 186
Hat in Hand / 188
Human Nature / 189

## Darklight

Darklight / 199
Hesitation Waltz / 201
Swiss Miss / 208
Dream / 212
Calaca / 214
Prayer of Initiation / 220
Accident of the Axe / 222
At Some Time / 224
Theatrical Story / 230
Standard–16, *I Remember You* / 231
Six Short Poems / 238
Border Towns / 242
Reversal of Fortunes / 246
That's a Thought / 251
Gallery / 255
Dolls / 259
Prayer to the Most Powerful Hand / 260
A Cole Porter Medley / 262
Too Late Now / 264
My Little Plane / 267
Roughly There / 274
Two Drunks / 281

Lockout / 282
Cairo / 284
Foolish Heart / 291
Standard–17, *Some Other Time* / 294
Feather / 301
Hooked / 303
Table / 304
Prayer for Travelers / 309
Moon / 311
Gardening / 312

**Death Sentences**

Inspiration / 315
Standard–18: *There Will Never Be Another You* / 316
Death Sentences / 321
The Red Ribbon / 328
Flowers / 331
I Don't Know / 345
After the Storm / 352
After the Photograph / 353
After the Concert / 354
After Long Silence / 355
After the Wedding / 356
After the Fall / 357
After Divorce / 358
After Angelica Waiting / 359
After Longstanding / 360
After Lingering Illness / 361
After Death / 362
Afterwards / 363
I've Lost My Whistle / 364
Disturbed / 366
A Wink and a Nod / 373
Child Lost in the Forest / 375

Etudes / 379
That Way / 386
The Meal / 388


## See / Saw

Bird / 395
See-Saw / 396
In Time / 403
Four Dogs / 406
Faith / 410
Skeleton / 411
Trees / 418
Wind / 419
Fire / 420
Rain / 421
The Sea / 422
Nature / 423
The Fall / 424
Standard–19: *I Live Dreaming (Vivo Sonhando)* / 431
Winter in This City / 435
Mystery Stories / 438
The Names / 443
Darkness / 450
January / 452
Hummingbird / 453
Birds / 454
No Love Dying / 461


*Acknowledgements* / 465

*For my family,
and always, in memory, for Miriam.*

# UNFINISHED BUILDING

## Rose Poem

Seeing the yellow roses along the fence
and the honeysuckle
and that around each separate cluster
    weeds have grown that are
particular to each and hold
tight against, but under
those
    strange guarding umbrellas
of yellow buds and leaves—

I think
the weeds may be more
complex still than are the roses:
the way they change each year
in color, size and form, and shift
their attitudes around the yard.

And what of the human sense in which
we usually see these aspects
    —though truly of another world
that we need guarding too
and succoring, as if
our frail loves
were the aura of an awning placed
against the sun, and the ones
we hold against
were stronger than ourselves?

These roses (truly
    of another world) are sometimes
choked off from their own sustenance
and the weeds, thick and ugly when compared to them
and the honeysuckle, take over—

but there is very little left to take
when beauty dies.

And so my love come back again
into some suffering
some pleasure and some resolve;
      the weeds are no less tender
in their need
even if they tend to overdo it a bit
they grow more strong and complex still
close to the honeysuckle
and the rose.

## American Scat

The crippled cat next door
   with his broken and paralyzed leg
      comes sideways and crablike across the yard
though in a straight line with obvious motive.

He's looking for my cat, who is
in most cases afraid of nothing,
chases
   dogs, people and cats out
usually, would bite a nail in half
were it offered,
   but in this case she yowls
and hides under the porch
trembling.

   The easy hypothesis
for such things: she is
faked out by the hanging paw, the foreign,
wounded and familiar
   (or is it projection?)

I remember, in a friend's talk, a crippled beggar
with no legs and one arm
   coming at him in India,
him
giving him money, but holding back
for the others he knows he'll meet
later.

   The easy hypothesis:
a sense of guilt
   (about what though?)

What if his money goes,
the insides of his pockets held out
   in his fingertips, and then his clothes,
and maybe he cuts his legs off too, gets
a board with wheels,
        and then
gets beat out of his due
maybe killed by the skill
and mastery of the other
man holding his palm out at crotch level
*now*—
   better to drop a coin into it,
you can't win.

   Ah, my friends
   it takes more days than we've got
   to get things finally
   together, to keep loose and yet
            move on to our demise:

the cows low and walk together in the fields,
possessed of a certain style they go
full up with milk, so single-minded it seems
   that the field itself
is moving: the way sky moves like a film
when sparrows flock,
the way the ice cap moves
quite literally
   around the pole— ghost herds,
and we, the riders go
together, in correct order
in our dreams.

Old broken paw limps in the rolled-in fog
back, into his own yard.

It's very foggy here;
its been that way, with rain, for ten days almost,
and that's why I think of Mexico:

first time there, to meet a friend, I sat
in a bar in Tijuana waiting, when a little man
came down the row of stools with a little box
with handles, stopped
    to negotiate here and there,
and when he reached my place,
said —very directly—"Wanna buy an electric shock?"
What could I say, but
              "How much?"
"A quarter," he said and offered the handles.
It wasn't bad at all.

    The easy hypothesis:
private enterprise,
work, and a sense of dignity,
but *my God!* electric shocks?

    (though it does clear the fog a little.)

The rich get rich, and the poor get
the by-products and the waste
  of riches, never
get the rich themselves
but the myth only
that the rich are also
poor—
    after all
what have they got
but riches?
   and magic stomachs
     and golden hemorrhoids

    and Lucite toilet seats
    and silent plumbing.

The fog is completely gone now, and I find
I have completely surrounded myself
with bird feeders:
grackles come, the cowbirds, some
sparrows,
    nothing
I'd built them for really.
Loaded with thistle,
the ones for the beautiful birds
stand full and empty, maybe
too close to my window,
   to humankind
for them.

And then
that in its turn gives thought too
   to all those birds in Washington:
the Mad Parliament
of Foul Play in America
emerging always as a standard of excellence:

   what did you think Mad Martha was talking about,
madness?

    The bigger birds
push out the small. The sparrows are agile though
and very persistent, and when
the grackles come
   too close to their nests,
they drive them out in pairs—

that's an American Nature Metaphor
and irrelevant—

it's the starlings we've got to worry about:
the false eggs.

       O,
come and live with me
ye little birds, and bring me more
than foolish and dull pain
for a public joy.

Fun in the country.
Fun in *our* Country.

America,
    sweetheart, you mad devil,
what have you wrought or engendered here?
It seems
    it's gotten into the grain of the wood itself
    I've made these feeders from
and the grain I feed:

thistle
cracked corn
wild bird seed:

Nixon
    Reagan
        Bush,
or anyone in that order,
foreign, wounded and familiar.
Each, in his own way
makes hay,
        and there
all birds in common feed
without rancor.

    The easy hypothesis?—
the cat comes again,
the rising sphinx or avenging angel,
and wipes them all out
fairly.

    It is a dream
of justice only
like all metaphor,
a correct world
in which
        the quality of judgment
is constrained
by conscience
we all have
    or would
if the world were straight,
but it isn't.

The real birds hassle each other,
the big ones kick
    the little ones off the feeder—
the catbirds sing—
    the sparrows double up and chase
the grackles off—
the starlings
lay false eggs—
the red-winged blackbird
is mindless, but very tough,
the cat hides
under the porch and shudders still
in the memory of that odd and pathetic gesture.

All living things in chaos gather.

And up
in a realm like morals above
    these small and subtle shifts of feeling,
hawks and gulls and eagles move
and finally
        Sky Labs, Ghost Riders, and the free satellites.

And then
that final reversal
in which we too are held,
    captive,
earthbound,
in dreams of Justice and Right Action,
relative, minuscule and passing,
in ghost herds.

Come,
let us go now, you and I
even into the bathroom together—

the great leveler, the place
of primary movements
and old jokes,

    like the one about cows
    sent up into space:

*the herd shot round the world—*

    a final and sound hypothesis:
a twisted history,
a flat dimension.

And when we lift the seat it reads
American Standard
or Mad Cliff.

# Clouds
### *for P.B.*

The cold cereal turns to mush in the bowl
and the rain comes again, only
a few drops at first
on the upright pane.
    The windows open and flanking
already run; sand spots widen on the central glass,
the cereal
tastes good: blueberries and sliced banana
and raisins ride on the mush,
                      and at this moment
I can imagine nothing that would not bring pleasure,
times even when indigestion is a welcome occurrence,
it stirs the body.
           Wind now
and complete void of ideas, imagination, craft
of texture.
           Mush in the bowl,
maybe the fruit falls in a certain way
in which one could find some significance
were the search on.

There is fruit
but no leaves blowing, in the wind, the pane
on the left half dry, from the sun
now, which is open again

burning the fog off. The sky's
revealed in its magnitudes,

these clouds.

But look again, and down.
It's not quite clear
but already there's a full meeting of the parliament
        tho, given cat and hawk,
it's a house of cards.

Jackdaws, sparrows, blackbirds,
even the mournful doves sit
        on the boards and take feed,
and that too is mush
after the rain
we've had and continue
to have.

    The clouds break
into patterns, possible
named shapes. There's enuf
blue to make a pair of pants now:
it'll soon clear.
        The sky's
like an outdoor movie, in rain; wet shapes
just barely glimpsed on the screen, in a finger bowl,
continue to pass.

And what seems needful here is a sense of direction.
How else talk about clouds? Methinks, I see
what could be a burden to an empty mind:
    dark, bedroom lace at the edge of shapes
    changing
    like some dramatic shawl:

all
we need is love of
what is here before us
close to ground—

        that may be so, but
I can hear hounds running
across these foggy moors
   in the middle of all this truth
(a likely story.)

The cereal is
almost completely melted now.
    the fruit begins to turn, and falls
in patterns from the rim.
                    The clouds
begin to cook and turn
to misty fog above the bay. I count
six drops of driving rain against the pane.

   \*

It feels like a little flower, she said
   (Anais Nin? de Beauvoir?)
I was alive that time.

You'd read it somewhere:
like a soft & magic flower pressed
against your thigh.
   I felt that way,

not like a bud that opens,
  one that's done
     past prime & close to death;
magic
is that it opens again:
    stamen & two tight buds.

The sparrows, huddled
under the feeders roof in fog.

> It is not odd to find, in winter
> 40 sparrows in a martin house
> pressed together for warmth.

I do not press
or leave a handprint on the pane.
I count the bits of fruit in pairs to give me words.
> As a cloud of anger or sadness
> follows the man indoors in a comic strip,
there is no way to name this matrix or these forms.

>   \*

I'm dead some years agone, the 13th day
next month. I might have said it that way
*agone,*
> and rhymed with something odd
and yet completely expected,
maybe *wan,*
so we could feel
the thought was all our own,
could sing primarily just the same
as me
  (at least with the same joy.)
My gulls float, then turn away
in fog
and with them goes
whatever compromised thoughts are held.
A song is a game of Spell against Ideas,
a drink of prune juice upon rising.
Values
are left to silence
unless they sing.
A man sits and copies the birds' songs in the fog.
He does it because his tongue
can try to move that way.

That is enuf of reason.
Hello, pulse.

*

But look again, and down;
a small breeze rises here,
pushing drops on the pane,
opening holes in the fog.

Our doves
with beaks held high
walk around in the mist.
                    The ground,
in smoke, reminds me of Brigadoon (the hounds help
the image) and I'm
speaking of warped love again:

that way
I make you move here
much like a foggy mirror,
every turn,
each strut I'd put you through.
        It's not your self I'm praising.

Could I spread
your body on that anvil I protest
is love of you, I know
that it would happen
somewhere else,
outside this room,
this place that now becomes
        so bright within its animal darkness
        it could burn the tissues.
All our wives are gathered in a fog,

and Christ! I can imagine such
    clarity of purpose from that vantage,
I am left apart from them
because of words.
               I see
the birds are climbing
once again. I cannot hold them to their names.
The changing fog is patchy. I remember
in a fog they set the dogs on me
    to bite my legs and ankles in Vermont.
I had a mother once.
I was alive that time.
It was
more various than that.

      \*

I lived a portion of my life—that part
before its end—in a sickroom
counting birds.
               My son would come
so shyly to my bed. I couldn't eat hard food.
The window at my foot, its beveled edge imagined
mirror of a possible life
in which my son would pass
daily.

  I had a sense of humor once.
Everything brought pleasure:
indigestion, sound of my son's
foot on the porch,
mush in a bowl,
    the count of birds.

And now

my terms come in a sudden rush:
it is a love of death & sickness he beholds

is what he is: an empty chest, a vessel
ready to be filled. I cannot speak

the vowels of our names aloud. I cannot
help but want to kiss & touch

the growth of clustered cherries upon your breast.
Each one was strange & beautiful in their death.

And in the morgue they'd wake him up
so he could count their marks and scars.

I was alive those times.

    *


It begins
    to come down
more certain than before:
a spotty rain you find
very much like blood between your legs:
the flower
petals spot and sag with dew, the evidence
of a femininity that sometimes burns,
the way drops do in a sudden rain upon
a sunburned arm
    above a cast,
a spotted napkin
shriveling into parchment in the sun;

comes down again
in a crazy cycle we can't read

although we apprehend
configuration of its form,
 its certainty. The birds seem
momentarily frantic in its wash, that
     rise and fall,
that shuddering in the wings
to set them right, and after a moment
stand again, resigned
and careful where they are. The window
fogs again and then it melts
its steam.

     \*

I left a piece of my forehead in San Francisco
and the good use of both legs in Vermont.
My right knee lost its mobility in Ohio
and I cashed in three feet of intestine in Arizona.

The skin of my teeth left me for a woman in Bisbee
and my faith went sour in Corpus Christi.
Bowels' juice drained out with fat in Los Angeles
and my right arm fell apart in Colorado.

There are wet shirts, hung
like sick skin
     over clotheslines in Hollywood,
my father's body strung like bedroom lace
in a walnut tree, in El Monte.
Hounds
I have owned still sniff in the shrubs
whining against property.

Tucson,
mother and I

asleep in the hospital parking lot
near sunrise.

       Inside
they are ripping my father open,
drop
pieces of mesentery into a bucket.

'You could have slept *here*
in a hospital bed,'
the nurses said.

The motels thought I was my mother's lover;
we couldn't get in.

I was 14.

Pissing in the empty lot, I watched them
empty buckets of flesh and blood in a trash bin.

We were alive that time.

I was holding
myself like a healthy flower
under the slate clouds of morning.

    \*

My dears,

I write against the chance

you might construe the fact

these clouds will dissipate

as evidence

    of a lack of constancy:

the quiet

certain nature of our love, our lives,

the way

    you press and touch

and cure the very skin on me,

daily.

    Even though

the sickness always comes again,

and stronger,

        all my women

kept my breaking life together.

It was more various than that:


I was alive that time.


Each one had the very flower of me.

I could not die

    until I died,

for living.

## Unfinished Building

    The sun brings forth
false caroling from the trees—the old fool;
a season in transition. And the other fools
        climb to the roof again:
a single shingle, butted in, left flapping
lightly in the breeze,
    where they quit it
when the old fool was gone
and there was a hint of rain.

He shines again,
sending perverted messages to the birds,
    whose songs are tentative—
wiser than he is, closer to the earth.
Only a solitary cloud, but a sheet of haze,
and close (and just over the lip)
thicker ones, and rain again.

It's the fitful start of summer
close to the finish of June.
A stiff wind rises,
    blowing petals among the roses;
their own futures in their sight now—
a symmetry around a center
which is dying.

It was a dark and stormy night;
a band of robbers were sitting around a camp fire.
The leader spoke, "*Jack* tells a story!"
and Jack began:

    "It was a dark and fitful night;
a ring of robbers were sitting

around the ring of a camp fire. The leader spoke,
'Jack, tell us a story/ and Jack began"—

    It was the hour (before rain) of a false sun;
a jagged link of workmen
were sitting around a pile of shingles
on a new roof. One of them spoke out,
        into the breeze—
torn pages from a book—
a bright voice, indistinct, and laughter
    (shingles rising from the pile
and shifting, the wind stiffening);
tell us some sort of story,
of prefabricated houses
before it rains;
of nail guns, a power saw, the way the rafters
are jacked up by a crane,
    the house rising
in a single day, and Jack began:

"It was a tedious night of group therapy in Boston;
no propriety for cocaine, but the marijuana
    (oil, thick in our hair) perverted us to insight.
We were a group of fabricated thinkers,
sitting in a ring around a table
aflame with roses; some had
    buds in their hair. I was hooked in,
wired in, to thoughts about building:
everything
on center, each stud,
and flashing in the cheeks…"

    I gathered the torn pages from the air,
and they were scrambling
down from the peak, and it was raining.

The rain wets the petals, a few
cling to the split rail;
      the pink and devastated roses
rise along the post:
a symmetry
around a center, which is dying.

It was a clear and lazy day in Savannah—
up North it was raining.
A band of casual acquaintances
    were gathered around each other, walking.
There was a fleamarket:
      old tools, glass roses and flashing.
Moss hung in the small parks,
Spanish restaurants, awkward in their architecture.
Somebody told a quick story,
soon forgotten.

Then came upon the house shell
and entered it.
   It had once been three stories;
and could see the notches in the brick,
rhythmic, and rising
where the beams had been set.
         There were trees dancing,
waving, in the empty frames, shifting shadows.
All the notches were perfect, true
and symmetrical
to the high ceiling.

Up North it was raining, water bleeding
along shingles
in the cheeks of false chimneys.
I lifted
the assembled book and smelled the pages.

But the roses! I was listening
to Bird across the water from Boston.
   It was a dark and stormy night,
but the band held
the station
            (a camp fire in the hearth).
I had salvaged two buds and a firecracker
honeysuckle more dramatic,
and one full bloom—already
pink petals
gathered around the small blue vase;

   Bird on the water, stormy
on a stormy night:
the dead sing better than the living.

The old fool is out again.
   The birds are unconvinced; only
a young sparrow tests him
swelling, on pine's limb, and facing him.

The young fools
stand at the flimsy walls (the sheets of mock cedar)
testing the breeze, turning in a small band,
laughing and joking.
   As the breeze shifts, from bay to backside,
I can hear them. One reaches for a headband
and adjusts it (a sweat or rain band):
I can make nothing out.

It was a dark and stormy night.
A band of arsonists were sitting around a camp fire
   in a cozy house shell in Savannah,
the leader spoke, "*Jack*, feed the fire."
And Jack began.

       The studs were thin kindling, the beams,
bowed from the span,
were cracked against his knee;
he crushed chunks of subflooring in his hands.
The leader spoke, picking his teeth
    with a post, "Jack, tell us a story!"
And Jack began.

       "It was summer, and the wild
wood was bleeding;
    amber of pine sap,
dark shadows of tree cutters in the forest.
One of them carried the work-load chit—
anything would do:
they could grind and press it,
call it board. The suns
        branch-cut beams
lay in patterns on the sticky bark,
then faded: a storm was coming.
    (Down South it was mild and sunny.)
And they killed a tree
and built a smoky camp fire
from the raw wood."

But the roses! The dark
    and sweet smell of the fallen petals!
To keep the fool off,
I wet and stick one on my nose.
Thorns hold out stronger than standard nails;
a line of red sap, oozing
along my arm.

The birds are singing, the pines
full now,
a band of sparrows

in crooked chain on a thin limb.
        Dull thunk of the nail gun;
they're up on the roof again.

I had imagined rain.
I had imagined the moon setting
        the needle on center again,
unwavering, the day moon—
the sun brash and inconstant—
        the birds answering only to the moon,
even the night birds
in the day light.

        I had imagined Savannah—
the house shell—my brother, Jack
in Wisconsin,
        mild and sunny down South,
a dark storm in the North:
a dead player, but a live saxophone
across the water.

I had been thinking about roses;
the way the house
        rose in the distance,
petals, and rows of sparrows.

Jack rows to the center
        of the flat mountain lake;
the bird is an osprey,
his voice screams on the water; he reconstructs
a crane in a bare tree;
        the crane is screaming, the tree shaking,
but the crane's house holds,
shudders, and holds.
        "Jack, tell us a story!"

And Jack began with a storm,
    fishing in high country
miles in.
It was crisp and clear, a blue sky,
    and rose at the tree tips like fire.
He was intent on the water,
until the water darkened: a sudden rain,
and then thunder and more rain,
and the trail flooded.

It rained for two days;
       there was a constant and stiff wind.
He built a lean-to against trees
*in* the rain, managed a small camp fire,
and stayed dry.

When the rain stopped, he came out.
It was a dark and stormy night,
    but there was a full moon.

He found he had built his house
against a tree
in which there was the tight, dry house
of an osprey.
That was the story.

Underneath this story:
    It was a bright night of remembrance in Boston
which is recorded, like therapy
in pages gathered—as if petals—into a book.
       Maybe it was not that:
Savannah? Wisconsin? a saxophone?

It could have been
a band of children sitting around a camp fire—

Pepperdine, the Boy Scouts, 1947—
    twisting plastic strands
into lanyards: everyone to have a whistle
for warning, keeping the household ghosts off,
possible tent fires.

The leader spoke, "Jack, tell us a ghost story,"
but Jack was missing.
We found him
snug, in the log house,
writing.

    And for punishment:
to build a small cabin with Lincoln Logs,
to true up each angle,
doorway and frame. In a window,
on a small chair, he put a saxophone;
    there were shingles, a stoop,
a stone chimney—
    a wonder of ingenuity—
emblem of the country: tight fitted notches.

And the leader stood
straight on the caps at the peak, half mesmerized,
looking out the window and across the water
    (at Boston? Savannah? Wisconsin?);
the house held, and Jack began:

It was a dark and stormy night.
A band of robbers were sitting around a camp fire.
The leader spoke, "*Jack* tells a story!"
And Jack began—

    and the story unpeeled like a sheath
of onionskin paper, a book

made of pulp in Savannah, from wood cut
in Wisconsin, sold in Boston—
   of fine trees used to make saxophone reeds;
there was no moon, but band held bars
of Bird over the water,
        the bright bay,
and over the Bird, dark clouds:
unexplainable rose petals on the bay's surface.


And the story continued to the first light of morning;
the clouds were clearing,
   and Jack began
bringing his head up: to discover
he was alone at a desk among scattered pages,
rectangular petals.
     The sky was vacant;
the old fool shone forth.


Out the window,
the roses were buttons on the stems.


And there, in the distance, the innocent house
had risen in the turn of one day—
   the band of young fools sat,
gathered around the false chimney at the peak;
they were laughing and telling stories.


   Their leader, the architect-builder,
was on the ground
standing among the discards,
hands on his hips, looking up, and smiling.


Jack could make out the songs of the sparrows,
the dead, alive in the saxophone, across the water.
   He saw the clouds

move in over the strains, saw the architect-
builder look up also.

Both Jack
and the leader knew
that before the day ended
it would be dark and stormy.

## El Monte

    In El Monte, the maniacs
ran on the dirt roads on their bicycles;
some carried the *Times*, even then
        the weight of wet rags
rolled into tubes: 50 or more
Sunday-onlys. Christ
    you're at it again
rolling before the first light,
 in the smoke of smudge pots,
apparitional brains of orange trees, a maniac
in California.

Freedom forever:
no excuse this morning; it was sunny at 6,
    then the storm came on, completely visible—
a blanket of low-hung clouds,
black as smudging, a line in from the bay.
        Was your blanket pulled
back up over you, and were you sleeping again?
El Monte,
a force in the lives of many;
where are you, and do you remember?

        To be elegant and straight;
to stand up straight.
To be relevant, but not glorious, invisible,
not at odds.
   To stand straight up in a crowd,
going unnoticed, but to go in
for a job or a marriage—
to be hired, above all others because
you stand straight (the truss

         forcing your shoulders back,
until it becomes habit).

El Monte—
that a man close to 50 can remember you—
eucalyptus and berry vine;
   you're turning in your truss,
turning the white column of your neck, adolescent
assertiveness:
   small chin, small mounds in the mesh,
wide shoulder straps
      your back like a wide
white board,
the torch of your yellow hair.

It was a hell without music
hell, of the twists of adolescence seeping
         down into childhood—
did I hug my sister?
Was my mouth in that hellish O?
You took your white shirt off to show us,
told us
      to stand up straight (I imagined
to avoid such torture):
freedom forever from the babysitter.

Bellows pushing the blanket to waves, or
under the waves,
   white dolphin in clear water,
sheet caps at the tips; or a burial—
waves of the wrapped body
         under the waves of the sea—
waves of memory, El Monte: probably
not where you are.
      But what do you think of (a woman of 60)

when you take pause, on a rainy day?
Probably not El Monte.
Think of anything— La Puente,
    a town on the outskirts, a trailer park, the light
that is always wakefulness,
a musical chime of whitecaps on the bay,
the entire sea of memory.

    And thinking of you, it's a turbulence;
now I am too old for you—
still wanting you— this maniacal
pedaling fool.
Was it your father dressed you: white shirt
    and fake white pearls of his story,
a white skirt to stand up straight in,
gave you money?
Who would live in El Monte
    (dirt roads and orange groves)
but the poor?

And you *did* stand straight,
    took freedom from your father's trappings,
stood behind twisted
        net of vines in eucalyptus;
stripped to your truss—
wide, animal straps at your shoulders—
    you turned for us,
pornographic beyond the consciousness
of young boys who watched you,
at a good distance, smoking the vines:
        the lift of your small breasts,
and turned for us,
who were empty of all thoughts of freedom,
our mouths in those hellish Os.

And later, it was said to be
La Puente—
    Mexicans in the trailer park,
your truss hung on a nail
driven into a tree (I imagine
        free of the torture, a still
white harness in the moonlight).

And you are 60,
and I am still, at times, that maniac.
    I think I remember passing you, once
at 6 AM, in your white outfit;
you were heading home,
a weight of the *Times* on my handlebars.
It was cold, and they were smudging.

    And did you pause, obscurely, in the smoke
and watch me? And out of it
a tightening in my thighs, a thrust to erectness,
or have I made this up?

Your father is surely dead now.
    It's 6 AM, and you are sleeping;
here,
the bay rises up to whitecaps
in a breeze.

Why don't you wake up, wake up!

Freedom forever—
    we can go down from the mountain, El Monte,
from the twisted vines, and our memory,
into the valley
where all the trees are straight.

# Floobie

Yesterday we got up early, or I did;
you stayed: the quiet
    slopes of your body still covered,
a little private talk.

And when you got up, I heard you
(was sanding in the basement) and was
        thrown for a minute—
what was that sound?
Why is it
leaving a place or coming
things impinge in their quiet complexities
on us?

    *(floobie)*

You were tinkering around with the coffee;
   I was sanding
and heard the unspecifiable sound as *floobie*
and touched the objects I was working with
fresh again. Why
in the bodies of concrete things, such identifications?
        The way
the paper becomes impacted slowly
as one is sanding;
   wood gives
      up under its roughness,
the burled grain, the paper
finally sliding easier,
pores of the hand loaded,
the job finished as the friction quits:
hand in wood.

*floobie*
into *shoobie-do.*

Well, it was old times, the sound
was a piece of performance,
a friend's name
    before he was a friend
but was close to others
who are friends,

and I was sanding
the wood forward
*floobie* & backward *floobie-do.*

Armand, i.e.
scat-singer (but that was in another time
& life), now poet, translator, friend,
student, possible divorcee
    or fatherless child.

Why is it
such categories, such lack of tooth
like the sanded wood, the screws
countersunk
    and hidden.

Floobie
is an Indian name, the occasion
witnessed
as He-Who-Runs-Quick-To-Battle (or)
    The-One-Who-Laughs-All-The-Time
until
he stops doing that.

And we leave that (still wanting it)
   take the names of fathers
      some other relative
grow
into false histories.

The family tree
is bilateral, one trunked, the way
the world seems
outside:
      birds-animals-ourselves,
but inside
a lack of such symmetry;

only the simplest natural things
show us the human face,
transparent, we think we have.

You
placed or rattled something;
It was early morning;
    I was thinking;
I kept sanding,

and *there's* a history: bookcase making
for a corner for you
to work in
your world full of associations—
our move from the City, your achievement,
love, a wish to be otherwise,
books & discovery.

—One
   learns something; that
   always feels at first as if

  one's lost something—
   (that's,
   a little roughly,
   from Shaw).

I don't know,
maybe it's
Things—
not
the possession
of them
  but the living
with them, the subtle absorption until
one moves, and things come out of closets
and we see we don't own them
because they are
not things
but associations,
  nothing
is brute fact, why is it
one loses oneself within them?

It may
be empty is alive. Maybe Floobie
is a thing he did
  and does and will do
again, and we too
will do our own names, like
"She-Who-Rattles-Things"
"He-Who-Sands-Wood-In-The-Basement."

I don't
  know. Sure it's a hard road.
But while I was below you sanding

you made the sound *floobie*,
you were unaware of? an accident?

who knows? Maybe things'll accomplish themselves
with a new regard:
like the sound you made
took me out of myself
    into somebody else's past
and brought me my own present

unexplainable, delicate & certain
Floobie—
    *shoobie-do.*

## Tide Trail

It's not as if
the trail we walked on
took us anywhere: we came
   to the edge of the continent,
waded, and looked around a while
and then were homebound.

   But the trail of sand
became a river as the sea came in,
and there were small fish swimming
trapped, between the boards that marked it
when it was a trail,
and we walked among them
and you caught one in your hand.

Julian—
this is for the tides of our lives of course,
that we can hold them recessional sometimes
and pick and examine their values:
   sandblasted shells and driftwood,
soon enough lost, and probably
more subtle
and beautiful when the tide comes in
to claim them again.

But now I am working too hard at the facts,
and as the trail deepened
it was really
Kathy, wading behind us
   carrying sox and shells and the objects
we might have left there
without her—

         who was overburdened
     and so beautiful
     in her rolled slacks
     in her inquisitiveness
     in her hat
in the sun

that I think I was startled to discover
(though not for the first time)
    the losses and traps in our lives
should we not live them
materially close with another.

I was missing my wife and remembering:
Julian, we too
lived that way once.

Leaving
the trail flooded with fish,
we entered the forest beyond it;
there was some shade there
and a bird singing
    a complex and beautiful song;
we saw, but could not identify.

I was still lonely, but not for the past anymore;
the flats behind us
    were by this time under the sea.
We were now together in the forest.
Kathy was curious about the flowers.

## Come Here

The house sits on the bay's edge, has
large wings we don't see
   in the relatively unassuming nature of
its low-profile presence there.
It's a half mile away.
You're 300
having left yesterday,
gone down to the city for library work
and I'm alone here.

Our cat
was bothering me last night looking for you.
I saw the man who owns the house
the first time this summer
   on his private road, and the white dog he has
for style
running across the moors last night
in a light fog.

It's all right: I painted a little
and bought
   and potted a new plant for you
yesterday. After you'd gone
these things happened
but now it's morning, and I've
little to do.

     No crest of wave, hardly
any part of the bay at all
is visible: its a foggy day. I sit and think
of fog in another time
and place far less immediate (but
that I think of it).

It was
a snow fog
adrift in the hilly streets, and we
walked in the Arizona snow together—
   night of the first high school dance with her—
She was Mary Lou, her father
was away in Texas
and we
held hands together
in her coat pocket.

   O, that rich passage in agony:
she ragged me
carefully;
I never even got a kiss from her
until the day she left for Texas
and that briefly,
turned
her cheek to me
at the last moment—

   was that love?

Above
The bay at horizon the new clouds
seem to meet the ocean.
The Karok
have it there is a place there
of passage,
   and if
one is pure of heart and chosen
one goes there
and does a life-renewing dance.
   Patipir (the flute boy)
followed her there.

He'd come to desire her house even,
gone a little mad with lust.
He wanted to eat the seaweed dried on its roof.
   He called her "About-the-House Girl," and she'd
always loved the sound of his flute.

I
on the other hand
went down to the Mexican border
   Naco, the Casa Blanca—
The one I loved there
stood in the yard looking at me, saying
"come here"
   (was about 16)
and when I got close to her
she whispered into my ear
"come here":
   I went there
and I forgot Mary Lou,
was cured, as if
*that* was love.

No crest of wave, no crack of entrance
into those worlds
   and dancing on the earth here will not
settle it: the flood comes on anyway,
is the dull flood of temporary loss, i.e.,
no flood of tears.

This
is not manifestation of love,
but lack of sufficiency
of self, habit & dependency
having lived together

   almost 10 years, lest
that be love.

Well,
the surf's burning the fog off
revealing the flat surface of sea again,
the bay's curve,
and the practicality of distant
fishing boats,
         and we
  see less than we thought to find there
  when it was foggy.
The house is revealed as a kind of money.
Love is a tricky mystery.

   I read a book;
Thoreau
musing among the primitives on Cape Cod, made
his progress walking along the beach,
would come
a little inland
to find talk and then
return to the sea again. Those

   land stories of dead times,
(very quaint) but what he says of the beach edge
seems still true:

"I used to see packs of half-wild dogs haunting
the lonely beach on the south shore
of Staten Island…
for the sake of carrion there
cast up."

    Bread on the waters? yes;

deer have more than hunters to fear,
they've
   their own world:
the dogs hunt and harry them until
they become hot and frantic
and spill into the ponds
where they are mired.

And one buck swam
straight into calm Atlantic dusk;
against horizon, a silhouette of antlers gone
into the Karok Gap,
   and the dogs panting on the beach, saying
"come here, come here"—

this, too,
was a kind of love.

A book and a few stories, the fog
coming
   like low clouds this time;
a weather like memory:
it seems clear
and then
closes again
   in intensity—until
Dog & Deer, Patipir, the singularity
of each passion and false loss.

    How
do I love thee?
say I am half empty,

see
the strange complexities of weather even
   as if they were here for me.
Let me count the waves,
sit at the beginning of all things future.

Love is a pain in the ass, but is
a strange clearing & mystery.

It's all right,
you'll come here again.

## Another Popular Song

"Heart is not the place
to sink or swim; that spear
with feathered dressing on its shaft
you didn't have to stick in me
when tongue would do"—
   I might have said to her.
But I was 14
and fumbling with myself at night
in relatively
chaste thoughts of her; so awkward
when I met with her
I couldn't see she understood
such passion.
   And she left me for another, probably
saw me a little cold and distant
and I was
and still am. She had seemed
like a little bird to me,
   but she was ripe for other things.
She could sing sweetly,
and often did it with others.

Love that is not completed never dies,
and though she is certainly
dead to me in reality,
   she stands up again
in the one who wears
red roses pinned to her hip
when she is sweet 16.

   I keep singing to both of them:
*you're breaking my heart*

*slow-poke*
*earth angel*
&c other popular songs.

# Alvina

For a while now I've had this preoccupation.
I watch even my flowers and trees dying,
and I have not gone
to books for the explanation,
the better to turn from it into some activity.

Caring
for bearberry and rose of Sharon
and a Japanese pine
   there seems to be some question about:
some say its old age that takes it,
 but it has to stand and be sighted
(some green still on the limbs)
until fall comes
in case it was Turpentine Beetle
before we can cut it down.

I'm sure this summer in the parks in cities
you never lived in
are the people your own age sitting
mostly amid the bright bloom of things
who are the ones unpruned and dying there
in the well-kept gardens.

That would be a place to sit, Grandma!
but the carcinoma has got you
down, and a little unfamiliar; at 87
you won't be going out again.

I've a story to tell you: last week
   (in the kind of natural light you like a lot)
I managed
to save two young kingbirds in the nest,

killing the black snake who approached them:
a direct and simple victory—

and that got me
to watching the hundreds of small birds emerging
in this birth season:
I remember
that you like birds and flowers,
and I've been thinking of you a lot.

That was not really a story—
but the point is
that it's things new, inquisitive
and alive
   that have means to bring you to memory.
It was always your mind's tree
I was in love with—
but love lacks
power in this situation.

In the city parks,
though some are wasted of spirit, the people
often outshine the flowers;
like root systems
they've no conventional beauty—

and the dying
Japanese pine
sends up a hundred seedlings;
what I did for the young kingbirds
was meddling:
the snake wound properly
into the tree's anatomy.

And it's August now,
and an early fall is beginning
   to turn the leaves off;
roots hold back
their dispersing of further sustenance,
and a cool wind blows rose petals
around my yard this morning.

It's getting late in the year.
   I can only gather and bring you
these few flowers
the better that you should live a while
with sisters that light the world.

## Standard-9, Just One (Some) of Those Things

The towhee sings in the early rain this morning,
telling me "drink yr tea
drink yr tea,"
   but I've had enough fluid already:
I couldn't handle that.
It's 5:30
and coming on: the windows are misted and closed off;
the rain hats hang with the sun ones
   though a little more prominent (yellow
and bell-clear) because
it's their kind of day.

Way down over the moors
the fog sits
   at bay's edge,
I imagine
planning that fabulous slow flight up here
when the rain gives in a bit
and it cools down
but the forecast says:
rain for two days or more.

How drink in
yr tea, coffee, or even a morning travel whim?
The day is so fully saturated:
it rained all night,
banged on the thin roof and kept me
fitfully half awake
   (though at no loss for a strange dream).
It is not good weather.

Wet trees, flowers, breeze,
what leaves there are
drink up
    and I
even fed the birds a little
dry seed
which is now rain-soaked
but they come anyway
and seem to like it.

Now
the fog comes in on little cat feet—
but that's not true: sudden
name shifts like the fog
changes the shape of things
around us: it takes time to catch up to.

    Gossamer wings of gulls seen
in the high mist and a suspect day moon;
even the lower birds are a little ghostlike
in fog—

and soon
that cloud comes in totally,
it gets dark; only the sharp twitter
of a pair of kingbirds
building a nest in the front yard, now
and then rings.

    *

The residual ritual of the dream then (a little vague)
in which the white youth gang was dressed
only in a kind of loose & scruffy swaddling shorts
& painted

in paisley star clusters
pastel, on one side, from cheek to hip.

were very thin & almost bald
about 10 of them (aged 9 to 12) dirty
faces & resigned & sad-eyed—
they confronted the black gang, who were
more conventional: black
leather jackets
long hair.

They wandered aimlessly
in a sandy alley until
at the start of it
somebody rang a weak bell
& one of the white ones threw some object down

& the two, some-
how chosen ran at each other
linked arms & turned quickly

& when the smaller (white) was lifted up
the other blacks came in
& struck him (had
kind of leather-covered bats)
until he slid down & then
they kicked & hit him into death
while the other sad
white ones watched it.

And I
on the backseat of the cab with Sandy
had my tongue in her mouth (the black
back of the driver over the seat)
& I handled her & she

me: we were very urgent
hot & ready at the thought
of painting
   this town we did not really recognize,
were in the wrong neighborhood & this
was the last chance before our deaths:
it was
going to be the white gangs turn soon
& the driver turned & smiled thru glass at us—
"You
should have been aware," he said
& then I woke up.

      *

How dark it gets
in the morning waking
from such dream travel; how real
   the bitter excitement; even here
each day a sort of adventure:
no mood to be counted on.

I wake often with night fears—
O Sandy,
whose face? whose mouth
   in which my tongue moves? were you
Rachel? were you
that part of my wife, my life
I don't know?

Well—

the bobwhites come at 6
in a gentle rain
on a very windy day

so overcast it seems
like earlier morning.

They are ground-feeders, and only
very rarely do they disdain
to land on the feeder's boards
and eat a bit—

today
they peck and look
and peck and look again,
the way they have for doing that
when they enter the cut grass of the yard.

They are dreamlike; I mean
they come close
are a little foreign and beautiful;
they stay
and don't stay
for long.

It seems like earlier morning (the dream
holds on) and last night
at 6 it seemed like dawn: the clouds
coming in quick at Coast Guard Beach,
that long
lingering aura before the storm,
the beach empty
and around the seemingly deserted
coast guard station on the hill
a powerful wind.

I heard
her voice over my shoulder as I looked out
turned, and caught her coming

around the building's side
dressed in sweater-covered nightgown
bedroom slippers
long hair;

a black girl
just in she said
to work the summer here, had
locked herself out and the two others
who came down with her
had gone to Provincetown.

And so we had to search a while
to find
an unlatched window
I pushed up and had to hold
and in the other palm
her slippered foot against my knee
and boosted her up and in—

   in the midst of which: her hair
against my face and recognition
of her withered hand,
   strength of the others grip
against my neck, the ancient
smell and weight and thrust of her,
the torque of muscle
as she rose,
   the certain
closure of the fog
in diminished wind—
until she crossed the sill
and turned
and from that darker space
   smiled out at me.

Every time
we find an open window or trip a lock
there is a kind of exhalation of breath
we did not know
we had in us
as if
the room entered in this
odd but totally proper way
were impossible dream space
    until the window rose
and like a vacuum it began
to accept us in; that there is something
almost clear, but fogged and misty in the way
we lift them over the sill, their haunches
suddenly very close and sweet (jasmine and other
steeped smells) and they
enter while we stay
outside
and turn and smile at us.

I remember the time Paul and I had helped
the female student in
in the same manner, in Aspen; she too
was newly there and had a way
of presenting a pleasant turn of body
in that posture;
we'd smiled across it at each other.

    But this time I smiled across the air
to the outer beach
and picked out a few gulls, windswept
but holding
over the shore's edge.

Now the storm is almost
over here. The two kingbirds return
to gleaning the long grass for food.
   The Indians called them "Little Chief,"
their persistent sense of territory;
they down grackles and other
large birds,
are known to ride on the backs of hawks
who come in too close;

   they are fly-catchers, and that
is a polished art
and a crazy thing to watch: an almost
Walt Disney sense of controlled environment.

Little Chief
takes ownership of the land this morning; it's almost
clear again; the sun tries
to hammer its way through
but it is not yet successful; now and then
a gust throws a few drops of rain against
my window.

I put a jar
for solar tea out on the porch; hardly
any sun comes through at all
and yet by 8
the water starts to get murky.

All these crazy things—

who will I meet next time
Sandy? What power's held over me
to force up
these strange conglomerates? what pained

and desiccated youth gang am I part of?
   how turn the body off from dreaming?

Love is cruel
and strange and a little blind;
   it has a dark underbelly
that cooks and is
too hot not to cool down,

   but it does flair up again
and often and indiscriminate where
it's the body that is concerned:

   whether in the backseats of cars,
in troubled dreams or other
real experiences:

it's one of the only certainties,
therefore unreasonable—
that
may be its craziness: how
bell-clear it gets.

Last night
I couldn't get to sleep at all
after that dream.
It was a waste of time;
   whoever you are
you were on my mind—
but that's fading.

Its 10 now
and the jar is solid and totally
opaque;

   the morning begins to clear up in earnest;
the window loses its tangibility.
I am
suddenly no longer
inside.

It was just one of those things.
The bird says:

      "drink yr tea."

## Standard-13, I Remember Clifford (From Dick Miller)

The gulls drift and enter
where they have no rights to go: air space
in which the boat-tail grackle
　is pursued by a mockingbird—
the glide and squawk, the beat of heavy
dark wings, until
he's wits enough to land, tuck head in
or quit the territory.
But gulls
have power beyond their age; their attitude,
　as if asleep while flying,
their stiff wings, is of a dignity
if we call that
being untouched by certain trouble.


I enter the bedroom; she's sleeping
under cover this morning—
cool sea breeze
after four days of heat—
　feet and knees together, that posture
we so glibly name, but she's no
fetus: broad territory of the mind's experience
I know nothing of,
and so I don't wake her.


Boats on the breezy bay this morning, drifting
as if a ballroom (domed sky); sails
　may have a way of dancing—
well, that forces it: a march possibly,
the way they lean in progress, tack
back, and turn together, in a certain kind of
timing, but there is no music.

I don't remember
Clifford, but Kenton, the table
at the lively nightclub where you played:
brash of sound
   mellowing into coda at phrase-end,
the two tried to dance to
awkwardly, stepping in quotations for a beat—
*too young
to go steady, laura, too young.*

   I'm in a dancing mood,
but she is sleeping—
territory
of the mind's experience
like a time in music,
I know nothing of: I don't wake her.

"Could you
play Bud Powell, play Tristano?
   Powell's still alive, isn't he?"
Christ, Poppy,
dead these many years: too many
       old liner notes—she falls
under the table for a quarter;
she goes down for quarters:

*that's*
in Tristano—
space of associations gathered
in phrases in a language. Poppy's
   under his hat's cup like a groupie;
Saul's face is reddening;
the hat holds back the chlorophyll;
her petals wither, and she's

under the table for a quarter.
I cant find the line yet.
Christ, I should have been a musician.

There's little stutter in the sun this morning,
few clouds attenuate; the smaller birds
fly out of the light
    and sit on limbs in jagged rows,
little zeros of significance,
    obscure notes on the bar.
The boats
have nowhere else to go, and so
turn again in files; close together now,
they're in a *real* dance:
    consideration of partner
in face of danger.

The joke was—
I can only play three tunes:
"over the waves,"
"stars and stripes forever," and
"I remember Clifford"—

    we waited for her to laugh,
who spoke of "Miles" and "Diz"
    and didn't get it, and she went
under the table quickly for a quarter: assertive,
but a shadow of herself to others.
    (Saul's face was reddening), and the trio
came back again
to the melody line—a clarity:
    divorced man with younger woman, insular
desperate and embarrassed,
a little drunk and disheveled—
and they played

*I can't get started*: Saul and Poppy
did a kind of dancing.

And you are sleeping: territory... well,
I've said it— we live in the bass line
or iambic: melody of the mind's experience
of each other, then we wing it.
   You're in a foreign field someplace
I don't know of.
I'm on a beach in California.

The music was portable, the sun
like hot iron in the sky.
   We were turning (on the sand
and the radio)
      searching for something, a station
to agree on. We found
*something cool*, Christy
   after Kenton, the woman
in the bar song
at the same loose ends. We sucked
lemon ice, and dripped it on the blanket;
our faces were reddening;
     we were squinting.
We married, and went
into a kind of
blind touch-dancing, awkwardly, and soon
   lost the rhythm and the tune:
the heat got us down). She remains
   that young fixture in the memory.
Would I
find a similar budding flower were you absent,
a Poppy?); how about you?

The sky darkens as you're waking, stretching;

the boats quit dancing;
   they head for mooring;
the little birds start singing,
familiar,
      as they leave the bar.
The flowers swell and shudder
in anticipation; clouds
attenuate, sun softens, and rain begins
the oldest (saturated) melody: "I remember"—

but Clifford,
*brown* is the color of my love's eyes,
   not those flesh petals,
black stamens: pupils of opium.

Your breasts are elevated in your stretching;
outside, a summer shower;
you return from that territory—
   dear morning glory—
not a poppy in sight.

And they were
turning on the dance floor; his hat
   held like a tambourine along her thigh.
She was younger than he was,
but not too young. (He would not
      play Bud Powell, play Tristano.)
They went steady in the beat
of *misty, send in the clowns, and*
*moon river.*

And we, the watchers, moved over
from our shared laughter to those private places,
   starts and endings, doors and gates.
Saul and Poppy

did a kind of dancing, then
turned back to back in bossa nova:
    out of step again,
drunk and disheveled, yet

in territory of their minds' experience
we couldn't know of—
Old Sun (till clouds attenuate) Young Flower.

## Shining Hour

The faces of four beautiful women
who sit in chairs, in the living room,
   reading parts of newspapers,
tired after dinner.

Their lips are slightly parted;
their lids are low;
   they seem not to be breathing
under the fabric
of their rough, casual clothing.

A man plays the piano, and enters it;
one turns to him.
   The light is soft in her glasses:
*ghost of a chance? shining hour?*

Then the eyes of all four are closing,
papers lowered to laps,
      food melting in their stomachs,
(those moon curves) under the fabric.

What does a man know, exactly, but money?
Their faces are not lonely;
they are not sad.
   They don't want money:
a circle of pennies
on my desk, *I see your face before me.*

One rises in a while and leaves the room,
and when she returns, she is crying.
      What men know is economic
or childish: satisfaction.

She goes to the chair of another,
her own kind to hold her.
   One is newly bewildered,
but the music has her. The men are fools.

Four beautiful women,
in respite in the music that holds them.
I am in love with all of them, and I have money.

The songs are edged with such irony.
This is our quiet evening.

## Here's That Rainy Day

Elegance of morning, monument
of silence, where is your language?
It is not
of touching: that is fugitive,
   and if I lift
and fix you
it will be in amber
      (a cat in the amber)
and that's pornography
and is not that language.
   Is it all memory? But,
carefully…
these are tales,
and it's the details are the substance
of all there is.

In the memory,
in a chair moved into place for you;
later, you re asleep in the chair:
God knows, there are details—
   traffic of voices to wake you,
radios (my irritations), never
metaphor, but images
and those seen now in the amber.

There's a house then
on the hill seen as the fog
recedes to it;
   raw, after eight years
it seems unfinished, while the larger
weathered one to its right
has settled in;

in the gap: nothing
but brown and green ground
and the negative space above it, of fog
obscuring the bay.

Memory)
without place or substance,
   you touch my face, my body;
it is an embarrassment
to me—
   touch with no future
or intention, as if
touch itself were the point.
Later,
it is a detail,
it is all there is.

The cat is dead, and still
   she won't go into the ground:
her shadow against my legs,
a whisper of sound at the door,
       (my father's image in the empty chair?),
that other gesture—
forehead against the door frame,
somebody's weeping (can it be me?).

As the world of the dead rises
in its pictures,
   to speak of love
in a time, later, is surely
pornography of the past, and yet
*white stockings* and *fat black*, the cats
come into the yard boldly;
   new pines stand in their lines
from mother pine: seedlings sent forth

in her dying.

Surely,
it will rain soon and darken
the raw house in the distance,
give it weight and recession
    the cat (as my father did)
go into the earth,
or become ashes.

   Elegance of morning, monument
of a deer seen in the distance
on the damp blacktop;
    I thought it was a dog, but
hesitant and exposed—
it was a deer surely,
a doe, crossing and disappearing
into high growth.

   And I fear
  coming to the subject too quickly, as if
this place were a gathering of subjects:
clouds form over the bay
in soft outlines above the fog,
    blond house and obscured ground; the fog
attenuates and becomes haze;
grass waves bend to the sea.
   The bay's breeze is humid,
though it is still June;
there's a promise of clarity and a sea breeze
after the burn—
then it might rain.

And of the flesh, dear Miriam,
the phallic flesh—

           it comes forth blushing
always, fearing it is a detail
(blush of its brazen youth
   in its wearing body):
wanting a language.


Could wake then to another time,
of promise and resolve—
   her sadly amber flesh that guarded her
from a wanting that she could not name,
in force of pornographic memory
      of yet another time: angelic woman
she could have give in to,
and took his hand
in marriage in her stead.


   Not these comings and goings, not of talk
certainly; possibly of song,
but none from that old school.
What is revealed
now in this new growth (after these rains?),
a quickening
that is a lingering, and does not sprout.
Though *in* the rain:

silent bone spur,
the memory's entablature on the column,
supporting
all gutted monuments. But

      what's this?: a towhee
secretive in the bearberry?
   my hunter, kingbird, on a fragile twig?
and over there—whats that?

2

Your language is hard hit,
so many details,
   *honeysuckle, pine:*
*Japanese and pitch;*
*beach-plum,*
and among named weeds a plastic
coffee cup, the hunter,
rabbiting, dropped—
   *rattlebox,*
*old-field-toad-flax,*
*ovenbirds & terns,*
*tents* at the ends of bare limbs—

it has quickened
and is not that language.

Whine and rhythm of a skill saw in the distance,
nail guns through shingles,
*gulls*, overhead, through haze;
   then it becomes *fog* again; *candles* dance
obscurely in the new wind—
a false promise of rain?)
though it is cooler now,
and heavier.

Wish to tell you that I love you.
There were comings and goings;
   it faded for a while,
but I was crazy then;

think of anything—
a sudden storm and a longing, a reward

as if it were justice, deer on the blacktop, absence
in the placed chair;

or think of those wooden fish in *Zona Rosa*;
there were so many...
how pick even a dozen
   and be sure of them?—

green cats painted on the walls of their bellies,
tiger tails! Some were a yard long.
Secret,
hints of ritual, saw cuts,
mustaches
   like some women, different
on both sides: smeared with dirt, but
     (lustrous!) even
pink underbellies—twist of a fish
coming from the mouth
of a fish on the *side* of a fish!
I wanted all
four hundred of them
   (were there more even?).
Just think of it!

I wish to tell you
that I love you:
(she bleached her mustache—
a small brush,
peroxide)

Believe it.

## 3—Another Shore

Did you have the eyes
of other women in your eyes?

It was a brief
sandstorm that touched your lids.

In any case, your blue dress
wet through from swimming—

did you figure
*I* would release you? was a hunter?

We drank coffee and were
soaked through;

later,
in the west amber room:

plastic cups on a glass table,
another shore.

## 4

Heart full, of nothing
   I can put my finger on;
the songs have ended but the melodies
      linger, like some standard music:
the tune's memory's fault and love's promise,
the chair empty of its history.

But have passed through
   all those seated and reclining figures,
and they're still half real in the half light

of the mind?);
    they're threadbare
as the worn fabric of headrest,
but they are still warm.

A false promise of rain?
*Lilac*, when the time is right,
    and saw a *jay* this morning
splitting a *seed*
*sunflower*,
saw *catbird* and *finch*
at the bath together—
    thoughtless and simple—
and should the rain come
it's no matter: *sparrows* in dark branches
against the wind's slant,
    and all the figures of this world
are perfect.
Here's
less than I wanted to say:

perfect). And so was I!

    I headed up the hill to find her,
holes in my underwear
    and in my faded shirt;
I was thin then and younger.

Gingerbread in the eaves,
a house set in the forest in the mountains
at the end of a long journey.

And she was standing in a shift
to greet me, flowers in her hair, her garment
transparent in door light.

No inkling, of anything but an entrance,
and she stood aside, out of the light
and waited for me.

I went into the shaded room,
and she was seated, a box in her lap, a painted
container, a cigar box, inset with hickory.

This was the beginning of the dream only:
   something to do with her hands;
she turned and fingered the box in a shaft of light.
There was a low, cool, fire in the hearth.
It was springtime, but there was a chill in the air.

And how account for the dreaming?
   I was outside looking for the box
and found it under a tree: it was a block of wood,
carved to look like a box, inset with mother-
of-pearl this time, and amber:
a block of wood.

Then I was somewhere else, in a room
with a woman promising things; the shades were up,
but it was dark in the day in the room
   (plastic glasses & an old chair):
outside it was raining.

And what was the meaning of the dream?
(dreams have no meaning); there was more of it,
but it's the baggage of narrative that I remember.

The next thing I knew I was holding
a cat encased in a block of amber;
   there was another image in the other side,
but I did not turn it;

I knew it was not you.

There was the empty chair, the melodies
in the room lingering,
   the tight smile of the dead cat, smile
from another shore, a woman
looking up at me from her knees,
perfect
and really dead. And so was I!

And in a term like memory I saw her reach for me,
her hand clawlike;
   holes in my underwear,
my shirt hung over
the chair's arm now: empty—
      I held
the cat in the block of amber
up and away from her, but she was not moving
toward it, or anything, but me.

Then it was *Maytime*: a tree in flower,
a ruffled bodice and pale cheeks,
   a dead one leaning against the trunk,
hint of a smile that drew me
to an afterlife.

She opened her eyes as I approached her
(there was a standard music)
and got up from death to embrace me.
We stood against each other until the blossoms fell—
   they looked good
on our hair and shoulders
but I think they burned where they landed.

   That was the whole of it:
dreams have no meaning.
   But I was driven to tell it,
perfect, as I was then
in that drench of blossoms
and those amber-encased figures.

## 5

A letter from Bob this morning
   (that's a memory)
from Hawaii;
he speaks of colostomy,
says he's joined a special club—
ha, ha—that has its shit together.

The dead speak out in the living,
and there is nothing for it,
no fear strong enough
to abate it:

   "I have no major
love in my life at the moment…
probably just as well."

Hawaii!
bright sun on the water!
and of an evening
   a bit of amber: a cup
on a glass table, another shore.

## 6—That Rainy Day

Herring gulls—
a line of fat unstrung pearls

on the dune;
   bits of the line rising
occasionally,
   and then settling,
fragmented waves of the line, lifting
and wheeling;
   a hill, and then another
hill,
and out of sight two more;
then a gradual dip, then dunes again;
then the clear sea—
   all this in the mind
(wash away memory).

A false promise of rain?—no more
   than a dozen or so drops, in irregular
rhythm on the pane, drying
   piecemeal as the sun brightens,
the glass becomes
transparent.

And in the wash of memory's
   dream of pornography and amber,
the cat's in her chair, in your lap
sleeping—
you are both sleeping—
and there is no ground there but detail.

The fog burns off.
The house in the distance
   lightens again and becomes raw;
the workmen are back at the new shingles
of the other house;
I can hear them
calling along the chalk line: rough bird voices

impossible to understand,
    but for the intent of it:
  the sun is out—the shingles
are still cool.

And so was I: that dip
  and flush of love could mark
far less—a cool
column in the shade, a sparrow's
sunny nest in the entablature. Lust
    later.

Off another shore,
fish swim in the shallows, close in:
   their fins cut the water
into turbulence and foam. In the sun
in the wake
they glimmer and have color—
are they painted wood?
are they inset with amber,
       sealed, against all opening?

(Grit your teeth): a colostomy,
plastic cups on a glass table,
  a blue dress wet through from swimming,
peroxide...
Here's less than I wanted to say:
I meant to tell you that I love you.

And now
over the bright blacktop
    (the deer's vacancy)
a marsh hawk rises,
silver, foreign in his singularity,
hunting (not ever in memory)

It s not going to rain—
but, over there…
    what's that?

7

You were standing at the window;
it was early morning. I remember
the light air
   of the space behind you
clear, down to the bay.

No one was awake yet;
it was 6:30—early for you
   but not for me,
for jays, grackles and redwings,
wave of pine candles,
brown thrasher and towhee,
    gulls high and drifting.
The work at the new house was silent,
the shingles even, and shining.

And I remember the air changing—
     invisible waves of the air;
a breeze came up,
and the pine to your side
   shook, and you shifted, or I moved
or the pine moved.

Then a small flock of sparrows gathered
and settled in the pine.
   The tree was behind you now,
and from my angle, the sparrows
     seemed to be sitting on your shoulders

and on your arms when you raised them—
the sun caught them,
        and they shone like amber.

All the birds were singing,
all the trees waving,
  and though it seems strange,
I think I was not dreaming.

The pine candles formed a hat for you.
You were in your best bathrobe;
    it hung, perfect, from the T of you.
I could smell coffee, and honeysuckle, and a mix
of pine pollen.

    The birds lifted
and fluttered, and formed a brief corona
around your head and shoulders.

Your hands were palm up, open, and waiting.

  Then the sky darkened,
the windows glazed over;
all the details of the world behind you faded—
we were alone together—
    And before I knew it,
it began to rain.

# HUMAN NATURE

## Sled

...and came down into the city on our sled
and saw a woman dancing on a table.
    Yet it was not a city
but a pretty mountain town,
        and we had come there from wilderness
into the gas illuminations,
where we saw a ragamuffin at the town's
gated perimeter.

    A woman danced upon a table in a bar.
The village lights
had cast her figure on a window.
We might, then, have entered there.
    Yet it was not a village,
but cemetery of a winter's wonderland,
        our runners riding in the history
of others' grooves
heavily, along main street.

Wherever the village ends the wonderland begins,
but it was night then,
    and the ragamuffin waved his arm
against our passage.
    Was it for warning
or tribute?
His wrist was skeletal
    below his ragamuffin sleeve,
but we were headed into the town's streets
on swift runners.

A woman lifts her skirts up on a table
in a bar, where men
    have turned to watch us in our passage.

Cracked glass in the window,
open to the pretty village streets,
	and yet we could not hear them.
Maybe they were singing.
We could see her skirts
	beating at her thighs in military rhythm,
though an afterimage only: we were moving
that quickly.

Where the village ends the day begins in fire.
The magic marker's
	scented with strawberry. It's a town
under the mountains, and crates
	tilt in the snow near a boxcar.
Did I say this was Czechoslovakia
or the memory of a book
naming a fictional town Černá Horna?

All night there are sleds at the railhead,
	the fractured bodies of children
riding down to the village
unmolested,
still in the scent of strawberries
and the distant music
of a big brass band.

Crates tilt in the snow near a boxcar,
	lobster pot buoys in the sand after storm.
The magic marker's scented with strawberry,
my finger, red, in the book's pages,
	story of a ragamuffin, nailed
on a white night.
I await the capitulation of the town's fathers,
a woman dancing upon a table.

...and came down into the city under cover
of darkness, but a milk moon,
       and there were men, on skis
in the white night.
            We could see the black
helmets, and flames of occasional fires
       through snow blow on the mountain side,
and the dim, rectangular boxcar.

I could have gone south in the winter,
could have burned brush
       on a legal day in the fall. But it's summer
and hot, and the iced-tea puckers the tongue,
as if it were the lemonade
I might have chosen.

A ragamuffin nailed to a tree at the town's gate,
his arm in the breeze the sled made,
only an afterimage in snow blow,
            glimpsed from the sepulcher
under the bodies where we still breathed.
Then we were riding down main street.
       There may have been smoke and stale beer;
the men may have been singing.
We could see her skirts beating.

I can see the sand hook at the peninsula.
I can renew commitment to my vows.
Strawberries in a bowl for my taking.
       I could have cut my fingernails in sun.
I hear the strident
music of a big brass band, walking down
            into the village unmolested.
*At some point during this time...*

...and crept under cover in the bed behind me,
    the cargo of her uncertain body.
I was the sweeping headlamp on the locomotive,
streetlight illuminations
    in the cool bedroom
and sky's
strawberry star fire
    on that distant wall.
I was wondering,
where are we going?
...the morning routine of standing.
    "Are you sleeping?
You felt like a stone."
"No, I'm okay,"
answering her breathing on my spine.

*I kept standing there without moving.*
    *I was waiting, I was afraid.*
*She beckoned faster,*
*more urgently...*
"You're not allowed to do that.
    Only with bread!" she said severely...
"I only take bread from my mother,"
I screamed at her...
    and went toward the door...
silhouetting the dark waiting shape
    of the gray uniform
skirt
and the peaked cap...
The others objected to this,
and insisted...
there were no mothers anymore...

...and came down into the blessings of oblivion,
the imagination of a sled hauling children,

a ragamuffin and men singing.
On a table
       there was fruit laid out for my taking,
strawberry roses. At least
there was bread then, some sort of rind.
It had rained, and there was water for mirrors
in those milky pools.
              Then we could suck at the snow,
momentarily, when they threw us out.
We were still breathing.


      I can take the book down to the beach.
I can watch children build cities in the sand.
I can wash away
star-stains
on the crates at the railhead.


           *...something about men—*
*and weaklings...*
      *the morning routine of standing...*
*but I found myself in a group that was going*
          *"on the transport."*
That's what they said.


...then came down under the sepulcher of bodies,
still breathing above the iron rails.
      There were horses, perpetual bells
at the harnesses.
Yet it was gravity's motor,
           pretty lights in the village,
a big brass band
and a bonfire
     at the town's perimeter.
Then we were riding down main street
on swift runners,

        a woman was dancing
upon a table in the afterimage
of a nailed ragamuffin at the village gate.
        The men may have been singing.
We could see her skirts beating…
something about weaklings
in military rhythm.

*They tied wooden boards under my feet…*
        *The girl was suddenly standing in front of me.*
*They'd tied pieces of wood*
        *under her feet too.*
*We walked silently in the long line…*

        I can close up the book and be angelic again.
I can walk out to the sand hook
at the peninsula.
        Red sails glow in the sunset,
markings of bloody footprints on the sea.
Her skirts beat
flames in the afterimage. Brush burns
on a legal day in the fall.
But it's summer
        and hot, and the iced-tea puckers the tongue,
as if it were the lemonade
I might have chosen.
*We were still standing there, motionless…*
*the morning routine of standing…*
I can be moving.

…and came down under the death of our comrades,
        who had formed, as if motivated,
a sepulcher over us.
We were still breathing,
        and they were the members

and mortar of our machinations:
    *thus did we see her skirts beating*
and before that our ragamuffin at the town's gate.
    Cracked glass in the window, and the men
may have been singing.
We could smell smoke of the bonfire
in military rhythm
    of brass instruments
where the night ended
and the day began.

And the day begins in the last
flickers of starlight on the cool wall,
    disengagements of shadows and cargo,
answering her breathing on my spine.
"Are you sleeping? You felt like a stone."
Someone opens, or closes the book.
The magic marker's
    scented with strawberry. Did I say
this was Czechoslovakia?
At some point during this time, speech left me…
    *I can walk down into the pretty village,*
*listen to a big brass band.*
*I can be moving.*
It's human nature.

*Italics from Binjamin Wilkomirski's* Fragments,
*translated by Carol Brown Janeway.*

## Spring Is Here

The moon is full. The lovers
>lounge by deadfall in the wood.
All the ships are safe
upon the sea, electronically.

I cannot see the ships, those cargoes of despair.
The lovers fight across the road,
>their voices flattened out
in moonlight
and the smell of sea.
>>Reach out to me,
let's bank the fire
and tuck ourselves away against the chill,
>white cylinder like moonbeams
on the coverlet, my arm for true temperature.

>That was memory
of a winter's end years ago,
strident still, and
>>spring is here
too soon:
cold clouds cover the moon, though robins
settle down
>along the entire coast.
O sentimental thing, those *Raytheons*,
the trap of deadfall in the wood.
The party's over.

"Not that I was a green thing in the house."

All afternoon, the birds twitter twit.

"I was once."

All afternoon, but it was night
and early June.
An ocean breeze had stunned them,
        blowing the clouds out, then creaks
and the visible shuddering
of the trees.

The moon was so bright, everything
        in sight: pine trees,
and you were standing there alone
as who you are,
luminous among them, apart from me.

How totally
I might have lost touch.
Loved your choice of jewelry and your dress.

Morning's sun over petunias and the bay now
and a glimpse of some
        navigational white sail
and black hull, delicate
pine candle's wave obscuring them.

What imagined cargo? Fruit
        or bandages: spring's curatives.
It's here,
and how think less of love,
        loss, and a little self-
indulgence
in this crowded burgeoning?
We cannot enter here, sentimental.
        I'm not a green man, or a green shoot.
"I was once."

                 Reach out to me,
little bird,
not my brother, but seeing me,
        goldfinch or black-capped chickadee.
Petunias vibrate in the breeze,
while portulaca
sucks at dark soil, creeping
        over the blue planter's edge.
There's vinca, honeysuckle
trumpets and the trumpet vine: these names
I am no longer among
and never was.

But then I saw you last night, alone,
but not lonely, apart from me.
There was a breeze,
        and I could smell the sea, may-
be the lovers too, angry
              in search of true temperature,
rancid cargo in those black hulls,
tucked away against chill.

Let's build some sort of summer arbor,
        literally, already winter bound.
The moon will blot out
              Cassiopeia's fall reversals,
that stone-cold dead reckoning,
soon enough.

Let's build it anyway,
        of flowers and treated wood,
our passions undiminished still.
You can be the director
            for my heavy work, and afterward
we'll steep in the tub

and smell the sweet rot of the sea,
then do that multitude of other things again,
until our party's over,
   as if in some winter
long ago.
Now spring is here,
and this has just begun.

## Collaborative Piece

It was as if her terms were wholly musical
and a certain harmony
        existent only in the past
had beckoned her
so she might sing that song again,
        appropriately this time, since she had
missed out on it then, was absent
when the others had formed their chorus
            secondarily for the dancers
who had gathered
center stage in the pavilion
as the audience arrived,
a festival of celebratory pieces
I remember now.

This was her story anyway, and rehearsing it
as if it were your own
you told me of your standing in the cello section,
how the notes had shuffled on the music stand,
        the overture forgotten in anxiety
as the dancers spotted for the others,
that you were grateful for the audience
chattering as they flooded in,
            though you were wishing to be elsewhere,
even here and much older, half forgotten,
only a storyteller.

I was somewhere in the dark through all of this,
and only now do I recall
        that wall of voices with a hole in it,
the absent soprano, and a certain faltering
at times among the strings.
Of course, I was deep into it then,

just as I am now in the rehearsal,
having her so present in your telling,
    as your scent and modulations
abide to be cared for
so long as I have breath left for your speaking.
In the dark, alone, and slowly sweating
   when the lights came down in the pavilion,
so that stepping out at the curtain,
    slightly disoriented,
I could see the baton
below the starched white cuff in my uncertain hand.

## Oppressive Heat

The stunned finch falls to bearberry, and thistle
    falls also, the other
        continuing in her feeding.
It's common
that a window is mistaken
for air, and there's a place for stitches
    in the businessman's brow, lack of flower
silhouette on the glass door.

It's the bird's nature to be aggressive
for her subtlety, the secretary's
    to be standing over him
still chewing her cookie in a colorful dress.

It's summer of course, they're working late;
the accident's industrial,
covered by insurance, the bird by me:
    rapid heartbeat in my sweaty palm,
light as a flower.

Summer: one of those brutal days, the air
full of thistle and humidity, and the mind
tries in the heat,
    the bird shudders in returning,
and the women keep chewing.

"Good God," he says, "What's happening?"
He's awakened
    by the patter of fallen crumbs on his chest,
thistle's brush against my cheek.

But the finch will shake itself and fly off into the day;
    the mind will free itself

and fly into the day. Perhaps the man awakens
to a vision of her thighs above her hem;
they fall in love, or he fires her
because the flowers
are on her dress and not the window.

I can do anything I want, until I awaken.
Light as a feather,
the day has no story at all.

## Moose

The moose we saw the other night,
        its nostrils steaming in the mist at Opal lake,
was not the one we saw
that other night, so long ago, in Oregon.
"They look alike," you'd said,
        Opal's bloody sundown glow your party hat—
you're the storyteller—and reminded me
of Hunters' Paradise and Barbara's apple pie,
        her evidence on the window sill,
the belladonna stain beside it,
after she'd gone away.

The party cooked along at boathouse row,
Mark and Judy and the rest,
        and we took a walk at Opal's shore
and came upon him
chest deep in the water,
frightened by that stolid comic look,
        his rack and trophy head,
and returned too serious for dancing
or for drink,
and when I left you at the door
        I didn't even touch your fingers.
Then I was in my own cabin's bed,
dreaming or remembering.

In the night, there's dry rolling thunder.
One awakens anxious to a thought of open doors.
There's wind in the house, a rising
scent of butter crust,
        and Barbara loosens up her sleeping halter.
Then she's stealthy on the stair,
        descending in her gown and slippers,

hair and locket bobbing at the cleavage
        as she's turning
in the kitchen,
gorgeous in the circle image
        of the Night Finder telescope,
still virginal at forty-five.
We were only hunting,
looking to enhance nostalgic memory;
        then it was dark and not possible,
and we were dreaming.

You're the storyteller: "Cupid's
        on the same page as cunt and cupidity."
Halfway between the boathouse
and the playing fields, we stopped for refuge
        at the band shell in a sudden rain
and wiped our hair and faces with our handkerchiefs,
as you reminded me of Judy's accident
        so long ago, that ominous contretemps,
and Mark carrying the bucket from the tent
down to the river.
"Give me only belladonna!" Judy had called out,
        startling our stormy camp.
There was a rustling in the trees.
Perhaps it was a moose.
We should have stayed at Hunters' Paradise,
        medicine behind the bar among the liquor bottles,
single beds and soft ticking for everyone.
The tent shook with her cramping.
I was thinking Cupid, apple pie, and virginity,
how I might be changing
my name upon return to summer camp at Opal.

Soon the children will arrive,
an end to respite at the end of June.

    Judy teaches lanyards and novelty singing.
Mark carries his balls
               down to the playing fields.
I listen to their whining
and help with homesickness letters.
You're the ghost storyteller.

Barbara's house was isolated in the woods,
the door latched tight against intrusion.
      But in the telescope I saw her
moving to the window
where she placed the pie and belladonna on the sill.
Her nightgown blew against her body,
         halter's bruises
at her shoulders.
Then the moose was snuffing
      in the stormy night behind me.
Judy sang
some silly song against her pain.
         Thunder rolled in over us
in Mark's returning from the river
            in the first drops of rain.
I wanted to search the house after,
give her a history of some kind to take with us.

A girl bleeds on the playing fields.
A boy has a dry, rasping cough.
One vomits in the van, already bulimic.
     Stomach aches and incontinence, a facial cut
and a twisted ankle.
A girl escapes to tell others.
Some wear lipstick, constipated in cold showers.
     Angelic faces, lanyards, silly singing.
Tonight we'll have a bonfire
and storytelling.

Barbara turned at the window
        as if in preparation for singing,
as if the kitchen were a perfect band shell
and the gestures of her open hands
could gather in the thunder
and the rain, like instruments, acoustically.
        I think I heard the moose bellow in parody.
Pie and belladonna graced the sill.
        She was full face in the telescope,
and I could see expression of the swaying locket
and the formulations of her lips.
What kind of melody is this, I thought:
        lyric of a virgin longing in despair?
You were soothing Judy in the tent behind me.
Mark was packing up the gear.
Soon we'd trudge to Hunters' Paradise for warmth,
but it was Barbara's house we'd be passing.
        I thought I'd take the name of some river
or a lake upon returning.

Now a child washes it all away
on a great wave,
        the memory of a day in the country—
a child no larger than my thumb
in imagination's rectangle dream image
behind the forehead.
I was on a farm, visiting in New Jersey, long ago.
And the child urges me in her ringlets
        and distinct scent
even through smoke across the party fire,
to think of it,
        proposing that we walk
along a country path again, that woman and I,
a wife I hardly knew then,
though in marriage she had taken him,

my friend,
      to find the better part of herself,
existent only in her mother's talk
of absence
and sometimes example, and the example
in stories of her once successful father
and his signature.

      We saw a moon crystal path,
swells of wheat weeds blew at dark horizon.
This was the great wave,
as if a grain field were the sea,
      and we were on the brink of it
and some discovery.
          "You know," she said,
"I'm not sure of this at all."
I thought she meant the marriage bed, conventionally,
and not women,
but we were later,
my friend and I, to learn of them.

Yet in that moment,
standing in New Jersey at the edge of an illusionary sea,
everything seemed possible without hesitancy.
"I know, I understand," I said, understanding nothing.
Ringlets curled in the flames,
         eyes glimmered like lenses
in Night Finder telescopes
    smarting in smoke,
her scent joining charred beef on the charcoal.
The child across the fire
was begging me now, urging me
      to remembrance of the woman and her resignation,
a man taken for the time being, anyway,
and no despondency,

               the way the path
turned crooked as we left the sea,
thoughts of my own life in observation
of the lives of others,
seen only through a distant indecision,
telescopic.
             Had it been later, and I Hudson, I could have been
my namesake river,
               particles disintegrated to a liquid flow,
passing all those figures of distinction
as they turned away at the shore.

In the stories of these silly songs
Judy proposes,
         women dance in fairy-lighted glades,
woodsmen trip over buckets.
There's a moose in comic face
and ill-fitting clothing, girls bleeding
         under short skirts on the playing fields.
             She brings in the past and day's residual,
a cut near a dilated pupil, stomach cramps
and bulimia, Opal's desires in the lens of a telescope.
         Mark circles the fire,
watching out for errant embers, curious tools
hung from his belt.
I sing along with the children, remembering
         a pie on the sill
and belladonna.
We were in the kitchen,
     sick, soaking wet and hungry.
You glanced over to the broken latch,
Barbara's hands formed a halter
holding her breasts,
then she turned to the window.

A rush of vomit on porcelain,
Mark as the mitigator only
of a passing pain. You were the storyteller,
I, before Hudson, the helper in homesickness letters.
            Judy proposes
those who are derelict and regretful,
a selfish maiden
      to the wrong side of the mean,
one who gets his comeuppance in the theft of a locket.
"Sing while you can, for the past
      is returning…"
I lift my hand in the firelight to stop you.
Mark pauses; tools sway at his crotch.
      Judy's singing
the song of a frustrated hunter.
Then we hear sirens and the sound of motors
in your story about that.

A woman lives a lonely life in a forest.
A woodsman dreams,
not far away, the story of a farm in New Jersey,
      another woman burning, or children
held in silly songs, seen
through smoke and detachment at a party fire.
          He wants the better part of himself
in imagination's rectangle
      image behind the forehead,
so he sets off in the dream's aftermath,
knowing a pie is her signal and a beckoning.

But there's another path
      and belladonna on the sill;
it's a dark and stormy night,
and the engine of his dream materializes
in the apparition of a sick moose in women's clothing,

             ghostly, possibly appropriate,
lumbering along quicker than he.

She staggers into a moon crystal path on water,
in her dress and tiara,
            heading for Barbara and the edge
of this illusionary sea.
He spies the apple pie, telescopic,
and the people behind her
pushing her,
       so that her arms
extend in rain beyond the sash
as the moose approaches her.
            The woodsman has his rifle
at the ready, the Night Finder,
       but his shot only accelerates her.

She drifts into the window,
shattering his dream, lifting Barbara,
even those behind her.
            Then there's blood
and pie, and belladonna
       staining the sill,
and Barbara,
risen in the frame, become a masthead
riding that fashionable rack.

       She'd been waiting for one of them.
He'd dreamed his face in her eyes clouding.
Yet he knows,
shouldering precipitous decision,
all the keepsakes
       of romantic encounters,
there's nothing to be sure of in this world.

The children shuddered in the firelight
in your telling. I could see
      her flooded eyes staring, those ringlets
framing her urgent face.
            I had scent of her, intimate,
as I opened my fist to reveal the locket.
Then we heard the sound
      of sirens and motors in the distance,
and I remembered the girl
who had escaped to tell others.

# Facing

All energy released unto my brothers.
Who is a sister in the face of my mother?
What father is released unto my energy relaxed in my
brother facing up to him, the one who is my sister?
Mother's face in my brother's, face saving
of the one who is my father, release
of his face unto my sisters, all energy
relaxed unto my friends and my enemies,
the face of war, released
in the facing of family, the storage
of bandages and bottles, story of my facing
up under needles and memory, all energy released
unto the face of my father, my mother
and sisters, family of my brothers, my face
in the bandages of memory, but in the faces
of the ones carrying my face into war.

—for the *AIDS Quilt Songbook*

## Heavenly Weather

We're having a heat wave, and it seems tropical.
The pines stand still in humid air
        like dusty palms and give no shade
and the women wear loose clothing,
men in plantation hats at the post office.
        Iced-tea won't do it, even with mint in it,
or cool gazpacho; not even the sea does it.
            What about sex, José? Forget it, no way;
this feels like retribution.
Even the terns languish on the sea's wake,
as I go back to a cool moment for escape.

Oh Mary Lou of heart's breaking it is done,
at least the ache is gone,
pathology on a snowy hill in high school,
my hand in your hand in your pocket
and commitment. How, exactly, have we changed?

One goes silently in the footprints of another
hunting pheasant in the fallow com.
        Only once, and still the bird falls.
Maybe it was all for love
and instant regret,
            your face a skull, and celebration.
What about sex, José?
I get sick of memory in this heat.

Oppressive heat's familiar to José
and to the woman
        in loose clothing at the post office.
She's Mary Lou, and Uncle Eddie
rests his pheasant rifle
        against the concrete drainage cylinder

where the post office was.
José offers iced-tea, there's mint in it,
and Mary Lou lifts up the picnic basket,
          Uncle Eddie following, eyes shaded
under his plantation hat.

          "Heavenly weather." It's José,
not a coin in his pocket, but her hand,
and they step down in sand
dragging chairs
and see the terns languish on the wake.

Gazpacho, in deep bowls, and cool wine,
José makes his moves
          on anybody's high school sweetheart,
but he's caught the metal
glinting from the parking lot, is turning his head.

And still the bird falls, love's face
          is a skull,
and though the music rises
pathologically, it's cool as footsteps
in an Arizona snow.
This feels like retribution,
but it's only Mary Lou of heart's breaking.

How exactly have we changed? Actually,
they've moved the place,
a leak of fuel oil in the tanks under it.
          "Just a building's distance to the left,"
the postmistress. "It's weird.
          You look out the same window,
but you see something else."

## My Daughter

The burden of enchantment comes upon us Angeline.
Again, it's midnight and crowded
        in the cabin's one room
heavy in smoke and smell of alcohol…
                and you are just thirteen,
but wide awake!: there in your glands and tresses
in an easy chair,
        long legged and languid,
skirts and seams in trousers brushing
your arms and hair.

Later, just the two of us
and phosphorescent
                crescent of moon
        waning—C you later—where pebbles
turn down under the last lap
…*both feet in my palms.*

Like a lurid face on a magazine cover,
        *it could have been lights across the water,*
onerous footsteps, approaches, a dark door.
But we stood in the glow of a porch light,
cheeks hollowed in fluorescence,
and below the gulls drifted
as if it were winter,
        squawks of aggression and hunger:
this picture.
Perhaps then it was the sea.

*It was close to daybreak,*
the house rudderless,
        though shadows turned and disguised it;
it may have been a river

and no sea, in reality, your mother...
Who was your mother?
              And yet it was that smoky cabin,
the men drinking, those women
in justifiable
short skirts dancing,
scent in a spill of Pablum,
*...above which*
              I'd winked down at you
fatherly: let's go
for lake's shore in the moonlight,
then turned in at the gate.


    (There were generous beings also,
Sandy and Margarét,
just skeleton faces in memory
of a past.)


*It could have been lights across the water;*
the bay's beach justifiable in the evening sun,
       a footprint of light on water
in the shipping lane,
              discernible motion,
and the beach walked at sundown for its jetsam:
       cabbage and green beans in a basket, nausea
in rot of timbers, and the early fishermen,
their lights too
       pathetic and mercurial,
yet stronger as sun sinks.


Sympathetic?
Swallows' silhouettes at cliff dwelling
in the undermined escarpment,
       their shadow razors drifting
below wobbly houses,

drainage pipes, exposed cisterns, thick wire
        cables twisting in the evening's air.
How magically the moon rises
    in these ruined eaves, afterimage
of some lost potential, suddenly
that sliver. C you later.


    *...and stepped down into the water, wobbly*
*in heels and adolescence,*
    *folds of her silk shirt razors*
*above breast buds*


*...but the new moon.*

*It could have been lights across the water*
*...her foot held firm in my palm.*

*It was the edge of a river*
    *yet straps of patent leather*
*and water staining*
        *her white stocking*

    *sweat on a nun's peplum, wobbly,*

*but a woman's calf and patella*
*...above which.*

*It was close to daybreak*
*...both feet in my palms*

*...wobbly, and reaching out to me...*
This can't be true.

A bassinet among weeds at the path's side, Margaret,
    and flowers grown up in the wicker: coreopsis

and a lady's-slipper, wild asparagus
in poison ivy.

I saw your bones from shadow at the porch rail,
then Sandy's skull face in the cabin window,
fatherly,
and looking down at her
        (lake's shore in moonlight, maybe?):
let's go.
              Then you touched my elbow.
Margarét, who was her mother?
Let's go down again
        in the lap of moonlight.
Perhaps
it was a river.

Scent of Pablum and dirty diapers,
smell of her grandmother's coffee cakes
on the sill,
then turned in at the gate:
        old man in the glow of a porch light,
and below the gulls were drifting
as if it were still winter.

Angeline, you were just thirteen and wide awake.
        My forehead pressed to the hard wood
at the frame,
        that picture:
memory of a door opening into weather.
It was summer,
        and the men were drinking,
the women in justifiable
        short skirts dancing;
Sandy dipped at the Pablum,
    *folds of her silk shirt razors.* Let's go

to the lake's shore in memory.
Somebody's pressing
the hard wood at the door's frame
in reverie, that's all.

     Sun rosy in the bay's waters now, low tide
after storm.
But that was an hour ago,
     the vague message always in the passage.
Perhaps it was a river,
discordant melody of a figure
risen up on flood,
     rot wood turned by shadow
to a body imagined there in sleeping.

Sun rosy in the lake's waters now,
template of sun,
     daughter or dark cistern, wet-work
of an animal hunting voles
at a path side seen through a window,
skeletons in a cabin;
where's Sandy?
     Margarét's feet in phosphorous at the shore,
standing over the body bag.
"Coo fas ter utter?"

And who was the man
standing beside her, those garbled words,
     and Margarét turning her skull in the sun,
shielding, this head lifted to see my neighbor:
     cabbage and green beans
fresh from her garden,
*wobbly, and reaching out to me?*

Like a lurid face on a magazine cover,
        image of a lost or regretted lover,
each memory is a stand-in
piety for you,
        each morning's waking
nervous to green beans and bassinets,
*yet straps of patent leather…*
        somebody holding a bloody slipper,
my coffee cup wobbly on the sill,
        and the finch playing her veil down
at the feeder,
scattering thistle,
daughter or dark cistern.

        Squawks of aggression and hunger,
a gull, on a post, at the pier later.
Canticles play the soft wake at the shore,
        a drone of detectives and forensic clicks,
murder, or the enchanted opening of a cabin door.
Sea, lake, or river:
*it could, have been lights across the water.*
It could have been this carapace of a crab.

Now morning's dream in perpetual calendar.
Now that the beach dies gracefully
        in this waking, offering
the prized object, jetsam,
or even a stone tricked up in salt water.
Who was her mother?
        The tarot cards fall for another,
meditations only for the converted.
This can't be true.

At the party the men were drinking,
        their black suits hung stylishly

from their bones, and the skeleton women
           in justifiable
short skirts dancing,
Angeline, in her flesh in an easy chair.
She was just thirteen.
        A knock at the cabin door:
*wobbly,*
*and reaching out to me…*
then it's the absence of Sandy,
        the body bag, and the bone stare
of Margarét,
perhaps … *both feet in my palms*:
hesitant, or delayed.

And my daughter and I
        strolled down to the shore in moonlight.
We could see lights across the water.

## My Son

A dream girl in imagination, certainly
    that one could smile
or place a canister on the shelf,
        sugar beside tea, without regret.
Humming, while cooking, swaying in the cleaning, she's
everyone's dear mother,
but for the sex.

Oh Carolina moon, down there
it was raining, yet a soft summer rain,
      and through the foggy window
he watched me as I cut her: blood lust
or boredom,
no more than a canister
for the wealth. It's Southern Gothic.

A son sires a son.
I am growing old watching Guy acting
      an old actor at the theater;
it's his part, and a younger man, his foil,
up from the South. But that was Carolina,
      and she was cooking chili,
my father's recipe.

In that moment of regret, I take him
      down to the lake's shore for reminiscence…
a perfect mother, days in the country…
down where he took the girls,
even his sister;
      one thrust her palms
into a starry sky:
all this prefigured in a magazine.
He was just thirteen.

Or he was under the eaves' covers,
        gazing in at the window
or down into a magazine.
                I was too old for children,
and to catch him there, then
talk to him,
       to say nothing
of my own machinations and regrets,
my active Adam.

A fire burns on the hearth in the cozy cabin.
My father sits, an actor,
              in the chair beside me: "Let's go
to the lake's shore in memory."
              His voice is mine, speaking to Adam,
some faltering harmony of ministration.

Sometimes the river is mistaken for a lake,
fog on the water, an echo that suggests an oval.
The cutting was an accident, the knife
slipped at the counter.
        We were slicing onions,
peppers for the chili, and saw Adam
looking into a magazine at the window.

Within the play there was another
            old actor instructing the younger,
until the boy was sure of himself in rebellion,
obviously: fathers and sons.
              This wasn't promising.
Yet the playwright wrote for actors,
and the play lived in performance.

Now I watch the figures thrown on the window,
pine candle and juniper,

sun's shadows after four days
        of rain in which the wind was up,
the sea lost
in foggy mist along the shore:
it could have been a river, or a lake.

And in the rain
beside the magazine rack,
I'd bowed over a child at the supermarket
        and stroked his oval head, then saw
the lurid limbs
of a woman grinning from a slick cover
that a son shouldn't see.

She was only cooking chili,
we were cutting onions,
        counting peppers in the glow
of a Carolina moon…
and the child grinned up at me, reminding me:
you are too old for children.

Yet the flesh is ancillary
        to the lurid picture, the sister's
a mother, or a dream girl.
        My father limps to the window,
"It's raining,"
        then puts another log on the fire.
I see her face before me in the glowing coals,
a kind of cut along the thyroid.
There's a knocking
        at the cabin door, it must be Adam.
Then my father turns
and waves it all away. "Only
a tree's limb" in the rising wind, and fog.

She makes a cup of tea for growing pains,
		interrupting her cleaning,
a recipe for reminiscence:
days in the country,
		just a perfect mother
and his sister,
palms prefigured in a magazine,
and the echo of a child's head
		suggesting an oval, a warm lake
or a river's
harmony of ministration,
down in Carolina, onions in the chili.

There was no dream girl in the play…
		in the playhouse there were plenty…
yet an actors' make-up vanity,
and the mirror
		was the audience, lurid shadows
on a window,
one's face in another, shoulder
to shoulder.

Then the old actor
		sires his son and holds against rebellion,
obviously, and my father
		puts another log on the fire,
only a tree's limb,
		and in the glowing coals
I see your face before me.

Sometimes the river is mistaken for the sea
in summer rain,
gulls in from the shore near Harbinger.
Report of a sister
		found in underwear

and gothic implications. Adam
    from cover to cover: lurid faces
of an audience or a mother
seen through a mirror.

There were onions on the counter,
    bell peppers, and a sharp knife.
She lifted the teacup to her lips,
a pause in the cleaning,
then was glancing out the window.

We were strolling
    down a twisted path, in fog, to the sea.
He held the crime magazine in his hand,
mine was on his shoulder.

In the storm's aftermath
my father gazes through the cabin window
    into a starry sky. "This is promising,"
he says, then turns in the reflected oval
like an actor moving
    to the dying embers.
"Would you like to tell me about it?"

Coughs in the audience.
    The old actor motivates for ancillary judgment:
suicide, murder, or the freedom of a son.
There's a dramatic silence
    in which the play is a comedy
of indecision. Southern Gothic.

Then it's Adam and I,
shoulder to shoulder at the counter,
    cutting the onions
and peppers.

There's fog at the window,
                    a lurid magazine
on the slick sill.

"Would you like to tell me about it?"
It's idyllic.

## Little Angel

"My little angel has a face
and hand turned
in beckoning, like a son,
on my shoulder."
Am I keeping you from something?
      Blown glass or
silver, only
some commodity, he has
popularity as medicine
      can fashion
dreaming,
percolating up
from day's residual.

"I left my purse upon the wall,
car keys in the gutter."
      She has lost her mind.
It doesn't matter.
      "Something…
in the grocery cart:
all of it returned."

My mother has an angel face,
cherubic vacancy;
what can it matter?
      I am keeping her from something
neither one of us
can quite remember.
      I'll be going too
sooner or later;
this we have between us.
Goodbye,
      for a little while.

"Also, he's a guardian…
and when I wish for something
and when I have lost something."

Little plastic figure,
        near her teddy bear,
my picture.
What's he called?

"I have named him Joshua."

## About This

How about this summer storm,
        the way the light gives back
petunias, luminous in casting no shadows?

Such common flowers usually, markers
only of a banal skill in growing,
then tending through watering and pinching.

Now, in the storm's sudden wind,
dead heads blow limpid, stuck to pine candle
spears, green thorns, holding up

        some party dress,
colorful jewels pinned to it,
crucially blinking.

Like your garment, that one,
some other morning,
brown eyes?

Tomatoes fresh in the mind,
red, even retinal, of a future,
and of the past also: light

        in the dead limbs now,
memory of a distant throbbing,
my gout-ridden toe.

How about some fruit, complementary vegetables
and crisp white wine,
a passing summer storm, out over the sea,

on a veranda?

## Cloud-Castle Blues

In the parking lot
      at the Orleans school,
the kids gather in brief sparrow clusters,
then head into the bushes, singly
and in couples.
            Drugs, sex, or alcohol?
It's hard to find such contraband
in those baggy Harpo pants,
      giving their adolescent horns
and chickens free range.
The rattle of a few
younger ones, this evening on skateboards,
      cruise between cars,
deep in a first fascination.
Thus do we pass beyond the school's activities
lugging our first row seating
and come to the old ball game.

Our neighbors sit in similar chairs and lower ones
on the grassy terrace, in a half circle
around the diamond—
           soft summer breeze
with a bite in it, late June
      and the no-see-ems are out, still mostly
individual, noted in their lazy stings
when the park's lights come on.
      We talk about that, and Larry tells me
about the farmer's market: plants and organic
vegetables, even organic diseases,
each Saturday morning
in the bank parking lot, just a mile or so away.

During a lull in the third inning,
    the pitcher on his game,
we talk about plans for our beach party later,
hotdogs and linguica, corn soaked in sea water
then roasted in the embers.
    Larry catches a Coke can, and the two
seven-year-olds
at play with anything that's at hand
are gathered into their father's family values
just a few feet away.

Adolescent girls pass by,
    lanky and a little hungry too
in their surprising hips,
this game no more than a stage setting
    for their purposeful meanderings,
no more than a memory device for us—
    summer nights in California and Pennsylvania
our common reservoir.

There seem to be children everywhere.
One, a senior girl, did the national anthem,
    belting it out as if from Phantom of the Opera;
    there's just a little whining
and most of the parents are loose limbed and easy,
men watching other's wives
    in shorts and tentative summer halters
in mid-spring, the women
smiling at their daughters' perfect legs.

Larry and I talk about dying,
    and I can see, but vaguely,
people gathered in shadow
    under the half dome
at the bandstand beyond center field,

the trail of parents,
        infants in their arms,
and the senior citizens, in urgency,
heading for the bathrooms back behind it.

The second baseman pulls his crotch.
The pitcher checks the runner.
We find the Cardinals down
        by two runs still
in the bottom half of the 4th.
We could all just wink
              and miss the crucial play;
nobody seems to care.
        It's not Saturday,
but school's out for the summer.
I remember. The parents of the kids remember.
The kids remember nothing.

A sweet salty breeze in off the ocean,
pollen and lilac in the air.
The players don't chew tobacco,
but they do adjust their uniforms and spit
        in that old traditional way,
              ancient for some of us,
and lights cast a dull abrash on the infield grass
just like California.

A Walkman-wired mad-hatter,
              brim turned like a rapper,
shuffles in a TV arrogance,
fingers poking out gang signs.
He has it pat
        as a music video,
though his strut collapses
in the girls'

        approaching grins
and lids falling suggestively.

He's like the rest of us then,
a little stunned
        in that half-womanly awkwardness
and stylistically
            disoriented by the kid
who spins a metal top,
organic farmyard animals on its side
passing in a hazy blur, as time
        sometimes does,
and takes a turf claim
in grass near his feet.

And we are leaving. Conceivably
        we're dreaming,
leaning back in beach chairs
            seeing clouds roll over us from sea.
They're thick dark and billowy, yet edged
in silver linings
at the interstices, wherein
        slivers of blue sky
and sun washing the gray stone of the parapets.

In this
gravitational reversal,
        we have an aerial view down
into the diamond courtyard
of the castle, in shadow of high walls,
but in clear sight
        from sunlit battlements,
where women stroll in fine lace dresses and tiaras
and old men sit
preoccupied, at stone chessboards.

                    We're tumbling down
through cloud cover then
and landing,
                    and perhaps we're speaking Spanish,
here is some other century
of a promising new season in triple-A,
though it may already
be a lost cause.

The Cloud-Castle Blues
are down by two runs in the courtyard
in the ninth inning, yet
            there's a man on second
and only one out.
                    At the bat's expected crack
we'll hear a loud echoing,
            sound ringing against stone,
to bring our attention back
to the game's ending.

We talk about dying in the meantime,
Larry and I,
            and sit in the sun on bleachers
and watch the old men glancing
at the girls passing
and the women too,
            just half-engaged
in plotting the next move, a knight
to a sister square,
                    and when I look down
            I see my little boy's sneakers,
back before that middle ground
            where attention leads to action,
out of place in a castle

in Castile,
never quite forewarned.

Why a cloud castle here, and baseball,
      but for the anciently decaying
and a game, as if on a chessboard, of recurrence?
It's all these historical vacancies
in the memory's holding pattern.
          Maybe the broad shadow of a plane folds over
              us and the ramparts,
the *Spirit of St Louis*, off course again,
though the actor's found his own
for a good ending.

The mind keeps drifting, passes
      left behind locations,
lost loves,
exquisite awkwardness
of a teenage summer snowstorm in Arizona,
Mary Lou, her budding breasts, and warm hand
in my pocket,
      embarrassment
in that communal urge,
          and a few family picnics,
even that one
in which I flew a model plane,
          no more than five years into this
in an old movie,
running through slow figure eights,
      wings above my head, around
and around the blanket
          where my parents sat, so young
and smiling knowingly,
life emptied now of that recording.

        Still drifting,
to a place of women in their underwear,
   an adolescent down in Mexico,
or those in winding sheets,
     the presence of the dead
and lingering dying,
   all these words
written on their brows and faces,
none of the I's dotted:
I remember.

Once again the Tea Dream rises,
   shadow image of a walnut tree.
As if originally
in black and white, then colorized
     through many plays,
the awkward past is given grace, a scent
like that in underwear.
So I was lifted
   seamlessly from sleep?
So that my father hangs again, his spider image
in the tree?
But that she'd blown the jasmine steam
across my dreaming face,
   and I'd awakened still in sleep
as well as waking, from the scent's insinuation
into sleeping. Yet it was the image of her
rising breasts and posture,
     intimacy in careful breathing,
what it meant to do a thing like that,
though done on orders
   from my friend, her husband,
after they had screwed the night away.
   A randiness below her nightgown still,
which I awakened in,

without a woman then, constructing
                what I had not really seen,
her mouth ready in a circle
I imagined only after.

What a boring world if one could right it all.
If she had been the woman
                I was missing, I'd forget her
in remembering
                a lack of resolution
in my friendship with her husband.

Love that is not completed never dies,
                nor will a song rise
vivid in the memory, but for a dissonance
in that initial hearing—lonely
in a dark bar, and jazz, perpetual—
                as much as death so prematurely in my father,
Larry's too, in talking,
                as we're stung back to the present
now and then by the no-see-ems, universal,
even in Castile.

The bat cracks, a Cloud-Castle fly ball rises,
two outs in anticipation
                and the runner still stranded;
our heads are in the clouds,
following its climb
                to gravity's reversal.
Then we've fallen into Orleans after all,
that field of play,
                or maybe it's California once again,
Chicano Baseball, hot tamales,
or maybe even Pennsylvania,
for all the difference it might make.

    Here, the Cardinals are fighting back
against all apparent odds,
though weakly,
taking their sweet time.

We take time
for the burgeoning all around us,
    thoughts of new pine candle growth,
fresh buds on the scrub oak, and the promising petunias.
It's happening all over again, back home.

Now the sky is clear,
there's a moon river over the lights
and the playing field,
    a pausing as the Cardinals put it all on hold.
The coach comes to the mound and they consider,
as Larry and I talk it over:
organic vegetables, beach parties,
death-defying treatments;
    so many options and decisions,
here at the end game.

## Angry Opening

Angry in that she showed up late for the opening
I mean the time waiting clocking buses along
the boulevard's uniform school children tethered
approach of panhandlers fumes and yellow cabs.

She carried something in a bag I'm a little angry
crestfallen her brow knit the smile I'd thought
for me over his shoulder fading and then gone
 I've brought this little silly thing she said.

I was waiting too perhaps a dozen uniform plastic
violets in my sweaty fist and consciousness of posture
tethered children looking up at me a fool for love
and whatever could be overheard in this diversion angry

but not now. For me? he says I was running late she
says and smiles over his shoulder at the violets and
at me his hand down in the bag to bring forth what?
A pen and pencil set   Cologne   A model plane   Chocolate

melting in this heat   Old Roman coin   Intelligent seal
of intimate knowledge in desire diffusing anger that which
through her smile over his shoulder passed to me in wait with
permanence of fake painted violets a flashlight in his fist.

# Old Musical Chair

Jane's fallen with a brain tumor,
gay in the garden last I saw her;
then she'd watched it from a window,

tended by another.
Surely, birds were singing,
there was music but it didn't matter;

but for work, there is grieving,
vines and clover grown among the roses,
wheat weeds above coreopsis.

Nick, too, in the firing of heart's howitzer,
how he loved this ancient war,
trickster in the joke of standard music.

Jane, my dear gardener, there's a party later,
but I will find the last chair;
nobody's left standing.

Difference joins the common ground, X-ray
shadows and his ashes. Say it isn't so,
this empty orchestra.

## Standard-15, My Old Flame

Fog trips along the roof caps of the distant house,
but not exactly;
       tripping is for trouble in the human case,
and the tall candles of the young pines intervene,
another metaphor. I'd like to light them where they stand
fogbound at the yard's perimeter
and have a lawn party. I could live along in their glow,
that languidly, just fine.

       I get lonely when the birds step forward in the pines,
"We are not your brothers" in their eyes,
and fancy the drifts of yellow pollen
as menses, as a dove drifts
       (like fog along roof caps)
from candle tip to silhouetted bow
on stiff, certain wings at five AM.
I get lonely in the morning and the fog.

And at that party, all my friends
in their fascinating ways
       and the enemies of my casual grudges
converted, all my lovers, even those forgotten,
"Here we are," and my dead father
and grandmother, and a boy whose name I can't remember,
though we slept in the same room together
under hospital sheets,
and I remember the pierce of a horn
that was the telephone
       and our tripping against each other,
half-naked at two AM.

       Everyone is still sleeping, most are.
I hear the truck across the road,

a momentary idle,
then tires' faint whistle on the blacktop.
We go into the foothills of Sierra Madre,
code three.

Carefully,
the candles come into flame now, with the sun
        and the first breeze of morning,
and the names of wild flowers, the last fog
tripping among them, start the distinctions:
yellow coreopsis, gold goblin,
indigo that turns to rattlebox in early fall,
        hush of seeds shaken by wind in their black pods,
and delphinium.
I'll never be the same until
I remember a few things.

        Exposed bones of her ankle, disassembled
on the street, and I could see her limping in the future,
regretting party time,
and my motorcycle buddy, ambulance attendant; it's funny
now and then
        remembering the southern vineyards,
a girl holding my hips behind the Triumph's saddle,
"Here I am," and then she's gone again:
attempts at love, pale imitations.
What was his name?

The day brightens, they awaken,
my father awakens.
        I'm old enough to be his father now.
My neighbor awakens, yellow hat in the garden,
and the day begins its accomplishments,
too immediate for memory.
        I can soak the potted plants,

pull at the clover that chokes the honeysuckle.
How languidly. I can prepare the building
of a bird-feeder,
get everything in order.

There were two of them,
one with her head in the gutter, the other
gazing in fascination at that foreign ankle.
        Both were in party dresses
and flesh hung from the spokes of their toy motorcycle.
              I remember him turning
to bend and throw up at the fender,
and later we talked things over
in our underwear on our beds.

        He had no father either.
I think I remember that, blond hair and glasses,
a night light,
        and the scent of eucalyptus in California,
dreaming itself away as all memory.

It's funny, now and then, when the party's over,
it's nightfall and the lights come on,
on summer mornings, late evenings,
        mind of a strange animal, that pathetic voice,
"Do you remember?"
        Lust in the eucalyptus oil,
half-drunk in the vineyards,
elegant:
        it's a sure thing,
only an imitation.

I'll never be the same, but the music is,
that sweet,
        Bill Evans' fingers tripping

in "Stardust" I listened to last night, my guttered text,
or the transported panoply of background:
    a party at his house,
mother lingering in the kitchen doorway.
I was with Fawn then, her gravity
        much heavier than her cartoon name.
I haven't slept with you in a while now,
listening to music played by the dead,
lonely in fog in the morning—
this added suddenly in the name of Ari—
Oh empty orchestra.

Wake up!
I can be insistent. The birds
    shake fog from their wings, and the fog
recedes to a background
at the edge of sea.
Insistent about the care of flowers, the spray can
and the tent caterpillars. I hear the slap
of a screen door. It's close to seven
and the day brightens completely.
Sparrows take up their mysterious work,
yellow hat moves among bean rows,
and the pine candles are green once again.
Insistently following the sea
    beyond fog at horizon, a beach blanket,
radio, and the Pacific.

It was Chris then with her bruised eye,
and that night he was the driver,
a black child under my hand
    and the oxygen, dead from drowning,
or was it that man rising up on a stretcher,
knowing his heart stopping?
    I can't even think of his name,

though I rush back again,
tripping in the gaze of attempts at love,
old musical chair:
        she who may in her immaculate wiles
have snared me
at least into sweet memory, behind me
on a motorcycle.

And at the pine candle lawn party,
close to the sea of names, invisible
at the fog wall,
        where anonymous horns answer each other,
baritone and deep bass,
I get a little foolish in drink
and imagining the presence of all from a common past.

We lift crystal and we lift plates of food,
my father lifts a boy,
a woman is lifted up on a stretcher,
        dangle of her dislocated ankle,
all my friends and enemies carry the chairs
and set them in a circle.
        Beyond his shoulder, where the candles burn,
the music of all past encounters, so softly
in the fingers of Bill Evans,
"My favorite things," and we have started our transit
only to arc and return.

Coreopsis,
yellow bloom briefly
        on the wild indigo. Already
she is rattlebox
in flowered party dress,
        soft clack of disassembled bones, unfamiliar
near the end of her leg

and fall leaves choking the gutter
                    where he throws up.
What was his name?

It's eight-fifteen.
Early morning's a memory, everyone now
in a sun hat and dark glasses,
and Guy stops by.
I'm invited to a party at his place,
          a house in the distance where he points,
roof caps a sharp shadow line in the sun,
the beach beyond
                    and the fog only a false horizon
beyond which some foreign land.
A birthday party for an old actress and her friends.
"Absolutely, no question, I'll be there."

Heavenly weather,
sun's rays filtered through a dark backdrop
of that final fog wall,
          shafts of light, as on some panoramic stage,
                    the sea, dramatic voyages, actual white sails.
Something about vague lust of residual memory,
each one an ingenue,
          some play about that.
Perhaps the old actress will be charming;
still her ankle bones are disassembled on the street.
It's still night,
          though the day is bright, and coreopsis
dance at the ends of long stalks,
yellow buttons
at a distance above wheat weeds,
and wild indigo is green, and yellow too,
small, sturdy blossoms, only briefly
to be savored,

        as she advances suddenly to rattlebox
and he throws up.

        It was the old, weak flame of the memory,
only that, really,
memory of the flame's last flickering
at the pine candle lawn party,
his name swallowed in the guttering candles
        as sun extinguishes them,
the fingers of Bill Evans searching as the game begins,
old chair,
and the music stops quickly
        as her ankle and future did,
and I'm out of the circle of the game
standing beside you,
        while my friends and enemies,
my father and your dead father,
even that nameless boy,
keep playing.

And I think then of the coming evening
(though it's only morning) and Guy's party,
        the aging actress
and the promise of her good stories, and you
and yours too,
to be spoken once again,
forgotten names and places, dead associations,
        flame of a life apart from ambulances,
California, and motorcycles,
equally pathetic and mercurial,
yet told into our future together.

The cells of the coreopsis die in the sun,
petals closing into slow fists,
        as they turn into it.

Wild indigo becomes rattlebox,
seeds in their pods shaken by winter wind
to remind us.
I've said it all before,
           different places and names,
but I'm quite sure you remember it.

How odd, dear Miriam, that all this
should end up being for you;
    last lover, close friend,
we have come through.

## Just This Again

Sister of bristlecone pine
I hear the cracking of your cones opening
      in advance of pollen
this spring morning: only four-thirty
and among your branches
in sight of my new neighbor,
      her robe blown open, white legs
stepping out through a doorway
to find the new day.

Amphibian as the lungfish, a venture,
male cardinal swollen
      in song on the wire, it's easy
to see family, though I hear she has none,
owns her restaurant, a business woman
moving up from the Middle Cambrian, latency
along the bark called gall.

Insects in my hair, your needles,
the advantage of stillness, a radiograph,
and I could be the Anasazi
      basket maker ancient as your sister
of Patriarch
Grove draining blood to ground water
in rites old as sustenance.

But it's only the seaside morning
place of America's beginnings, and she's
subtle or insouciant
      on the lost continent before the day
can weave us, and the cardinal sings,
she lifts her head to look,
and I'm stealthy as you crack and make pollen
to be used later.

## Remarkable Storm

Here, in the narrow rivulet
that runs along the basement floor,
juices of a chipmunk's body
where she lay in seepage
after some remarkable storm.

Days ago, in sun, I found the fetus
and the afterbirth,
larger than her body now
having gathered herself into rigidity
in order to slip through.

Earth's door at the party
under a starlight canopy,
the cousin grown fat again
neither in depression nor joy
after his stroke.

Please, stay for a while; I'll try too,
in presence of the scent of her urine
more delicate than mine,
flow of diluted blood memories
down the drain.

"Come again?" Just some woman
in laughter and music celebrating
this anniversary: "Earth Angel"
their song and earth's door,
for a while, only a metaphor.

# Wanda and I

## 1. Perpetual Calendar

A little light music and the persimmon
bring them up to speed.
    "This shore's a travelogue,"
says Wanda, "some industrial slide show
selling real estate."
                      Just driving along through California
windows down
and the top too, and Robert passes the juicy fruit
before the fall of *Oregon*
into some other Muzak on the tape deck.

How subtle, the state's rise into turmoil.
He had imagined ignorance
of the infrastructure, but that was years ago,
an economy of barracuda
        smoked on the public boardwalk
down in the heart of the middle thirties,
just wandering around, José.

Using methodology that doesn't include paying,
Wanda shoplifts in Laguna. She's seeing
a man who is seeing her psychiatrist,
        not sure of the purpose, but a dress
under a dress, elaborately,
a belt under a belt, and she's smiling down
at Robert idling at the curb
perpetually, her hat a short-tailed shrew,
a little askew.

But it's summer at the Tumbleweed.
I'm in need of a little candy, and Mandy's

unaware of our engagement, four rows down.
    Thus, the stolen nickel bar
and collared in the parking lot, my mother:
"Where did I go wrong?"
Oh lovely, little Mandy, hair like falling water,
    just a pin's prick in memory,
of any name or circumstance at all.

José,
    even in your Mexico, such beautiful women,
mother in a rat-tail coat in any place but California, here
at the bowling alley in Arizona
    setting pins; this too is gone
into machinery, the smell of oil and wax
and desperation of poverty
in your sweat.
    And did she think to drive him crazy,
utterly, or only hope so?

A soapstone at the motel, Wanda's
calloused heels and certain spells
    and Robert enchanted across the entire state;
chenille draped over chairs and hats and scarves
on bureaus, carefully, a gathering
of everything imagined, and it's I in transit there,
and Wanda only Mandy.
Hey, José,
I'm telling one of our core stories; just listen.

I went in search of persimmons,
    a little light industry and permission,
down to where a woman had needles in her cheeks
and a man ate a chicken. Daze of freaks,
    but I was in an age of bikes
and strolled the boardwalk alertly, money enough

for a foot-long and hot nuts;
and there was Wendy,
       waiting for something
I couldn't quite yet imagine, juicy fruit
and passage into a ride for delicate kissing.

This was Long Beach and the Pike,
       the late forties and the state
just rising into turmoil. I was in no way Robert,
though her top was parted to the crease
below which, mystery, so lucky
       that she had no friend, not Mandy,
and we were traveling in the tunnel of love together
licking the fruit away
and afterward went shopping,
       hungry in a hunger, never sated
at that age of an infrastructure
before *Oregon* and Muzak and the kick
       of drugs and alcohol
to get Wendy going.

Perhaps there is a message in this
after all, José,
the way I lusted for her body, indiscriminately,
each garment surfacing, as she grew fatter
       exiting the dressing room,
and I was wondering
about peeling, holding my persimmon
in the light at windows
for diversion.

Wanda acts in love with Robert now
and shopping, but it was I in Long Beach then,
regardless of her name, her face gone
into a travelogue, but the memory lingers on,

and finally we're rewarded, you
 in your poverty
in Mexico,
 some dusty angel
who would hold you, momentarily, away
from that machinery
and the oil and wax of bowling alleys,
whispering "*Amante.*"

Chris Connor in her song, José,
that portable music
 running in a sand river to your blanket
where they dragged her down, a few children
carving out her back and buttocks and her stringy hair
*when the world was young;*

 face in sand and fingers digging in, monster
of sea lettuce and kelp gripping
one delicate ankle,
 and she was gone into the sand's pit
in silent screaming, only a year ago.

I can hear the angels singing at the bowling alley.
Do you remember now, José,
 the senior girls, our postures
as we dug for pins and balls and watched
their ankles blink
 in bobby sox, a little retrograde,
their legs
whiter than anything in Mexico?

Again, I come to imagine you upon this eastern beach
after the sand sculpture contest,
 finally resting up from all that bending
at a great distance from Naco.

I traveled, not so recently, with Tenney
to las ruinas de la Casa Blanca, no less
        than the ruins of my own pathetic losses
when I feared senior girls in bobby sox
and took up with your sisters.

Only a pile of sandstone now, a few tiles,
and the figure still of that elegant
curved bar, the empty frame of a diamond
window where I sat
        and drank good beer
while you were shuffling toward the border,
a few coins in your pocket, and the moon
over The Blue Moon
        across the dusty road
also in ruins now.

José,
there's nothing of reclamation in this thing at all,
just Chris Connor singing
        *here's that rainy day*, a long way
from Mexico and memory of a bowling alley:
smell of wax and sweat,
and of the wood below their ankles,
        yet how quickly did our talk
bring up an angel face, that whispered
"*Amante.*"

It's Wanda and Robert then,
        a line or two, and a beer and highball
after hitting a few stores in Tucson
and a night of her unpeeling
in some cheap motel,
        enchanted, though he seems exhausted
and her balls find the gutter

even in that shrewish hat
she wears jauntily.

Certainly, he'll come back, a bottle
for the road,
        but we can see impatience
in her ankle shaking
under the pin frame,
        and when he does she's gone
and it is he, set free to wander
toward the border
imagining her half-naked
for another watcher,
        possibly a woman
in some seedy room in San Diego.

Thus, within romantic possibilities, José,
the infrastructure of the human dance
often to Muzak and *amante*,
still partial to that longing, whispered
into an emptiness
        like memory: the top's down,
the windows too, and there's that fleeting moment
of Janet in the back seat at Winnebago.

I imagined I could see my California,
and Mandy,
        stars going off in the sky,
but it was Robert, on the road again,
disappearing in the desert toward Las Vegas
and somebody's psychiatrist.

## 2. Robert's Blues

Pathetic through San Bernardino on a trip to Vegas
memory of Wanda stripping and her stare,
    having to find it someway,
that rise out of enchantment to betrayal
on a twisted road—
Joshua, dwarfed mountain pine,
dirty pancakes of snow at altitude.

*Oregon*'s oboe rivers spill through. In the evening there's
the Muzak of the *Alpenglühen*;
even in the highest passages in Switzerland
she's there, arboreal.

Fingers in my hair, Mr. Milquetoast
on the radio talk show,
        her scarves in silhouetted
passages of trees,
learning to give her up into memory,
    she who was no less than lust for music,
Dinah Washington's vague weaving
into an arbor formed of clothing and deceit:
"Blue Gardenia."

Damn the moon and stars, this
idle convertible,
    thick maple syrup over pancakes
in Kelso, image of a Joshua tree's gesture,
panicles of flowers in my hair,
the way she undressed for me in parody,
thievery of clothing,
    transitor of that meridian,
heart stopper,
delicate flowerpot.

Convertible's sandstorm in my hair,
pomade of lingonberries
        on my brow washed in her scent,
implacability of night's river of stars
and desert bloom,
        my stalk firmly held in panicles,
passing through Victorville, oasis
of Neal Hefti and The Freshmen on the radio,
Wanda wrapped in stolen furs
        at the lakeshore in memory,
all the frozen yearning that I have to learn.

The Buick's then a buggy fitted out in Barstow,
turning from beer
        into winter and Wisconsin on a swivel stool,
image of her bundled in chinchilla
seen through streaks beyond the dirty window,
skull face, snow-blown in a rat tail.

Everything must start again in Vegas,
        though uncertainly in her psychiatrist,
the giving back of Muzak and the grieving away.
And now the city's rise beyond
Blue Diamond, starlights of the city, and the damned
moon gone.

Maybe this is healthy, maybe
blue gardenias' petals
        in fake flowering on his table
is my plastic gamble, cards, dice, and wheels,
hounds at my heels.
Maybe now the cause can be discovered in the leaving.

Thus do I come to the emerald city of yearning,
psychiatrists and imagination,

many Wandas—
        "Can you tell me how you feel?"—
lost without her.


3. Just About Anybody

Muddleheaded in the distance between loss and wonder,
the discharged party waits for his walking papers
posed at the border gate. There was this picture,

buried with others now in a box under loose letters,
the idle snap of the tourist, Wanda, clearing the roll:
*unknown sailor in San Diego at the border gate.*

Beside the point of her narrative of that vacation,
a time dropped out of my life and into the waste of another,
jewels hidden among these photos, discovered by the night thief.

Wanda was chosen for age and imagination, that careful
wearing of garments under her clothing in shoplifting,
tricky dress for an older woman of such seeming taste.

A sailor, but I'm no more than a child in that picture.
Wanda fleeing with Janet, growing closer: a brittle
letter of old news, read in the beam of a pencil light,

a breakup, veiled in tentative language, unacknowledged.
Ice water only in the refrigerator when I left home,
found now in the veins of Janet, a thief of love.

Leaving Laguna and Robert: in that picture, really it was
Corpus Christi, come again in this dream of thievery,
and I was heart-stopped in Mary Grace and annunciation,

morning, noon, and night, my gringo Mexico might
just as well be Tijuana, so much memory is dreamscape
vacation, two respectable women at the border gate.

Take up these jewels then, the photograph and the letter
and another mailed, return address Las Vegas, ending "Lost
without you," sent ahead to this Wisconsin where I steal,

remembering the Boy Scout Jamboree at Pepperdine, the whine
of others calling for their Janets, and lift Wanda's diary.
"The sunniness of her extravagant bonnet, last Easter…

Hats over hats, at least a dozen silk scarves in September.
Chinchilla will be harder… Robert at the lake party
Wednesday, insufferable, but she was there too, in gold lamé."

Night fading to uncertain day, the stutter of aurora, hay
scattered in the frozen field beyond the window now, and Wanda
on a trip again, to Texas this time, and possible thievery.

Pins fall, fiesta dancers at the bowling alley, the rigor
of high school girls and wax covering our sweat. It's easy
down in the pit of this engagement, a dozen garments away.

José, the nexus absent in our childhood, your poverty, and I
at Pepperdine, though poor, in jewelry: ID bracelet, and a cheap
plastic lanyard—tenderfoot, your broken-down huaraches.

A sailor's discharge into drydock, mariachis, crossing
the river, begging for occasion, lifting silver instruments,
and Wanda follows Janet through the border gate. "In Tijuana,

her hair a golden trumpet's bell in sun … nothing of value worth
stealing… Paraded the promenade some evening, holding
hands like bobby-soxers, unassuming. Separate, narrow beds…

His *lost without you* letter, in Wisconsin… I have terminated
psychiatric business in Las Vegas… think I need a comfort zone,
an outfit or two, body layered for unpeeling… that chinchilla."

Ice-water blue at Pepperdine, the lake, and up ahead the Gulf
of Mexico and Mary Grace. How suddenly, José, the trading in
for evidence of another's history, a thievery, although

a picture of a sailor, and jewelry, letters glossing a diary.
This isn't really Corpus Christi, Tijuana, or Wisconsin, only
Wanda following Robert through Janet into somebody's memory.

A sailor. Poised there. And could the border be a bridge
to vague desire, rapture in her clothing, Wanda would be leading
Janet and the mariachis to The Four Freshmen at Winnebago,

a lake manipulated by the night thief, my Pepperdine: tripping
in his awkward lanyard at the trailer hitch, that boy, a gleam
about his mother, gone to memory later, come to steal him.

Just about anybody, José, could be a sailor and a thief. Just as
night gives up to day, the motors active on the road, my beam
fades in the pencil light and Wanda's with somebody in Texas.

"Giving in to summer dresses, that cute little party hat, coat
off a mannequin's back … still needing chinchilla." I leave
her diary, these letters, sailor's picture, take only the jewels.

## 4. Car

Sight of the kitchen door brings up
the scent of lemon and the opening
of the oven, meringue.
    It's scorching at the lake, a screen door

and the smell of coffee cake, my grandmother humming,
my aunt; there's nothing
like two women singing, be it Verdi
or the song of dead chinchillas
in El Monte.

    Twisted passions loose in the world,
humidity and adolescence and McCarthy:
it's the '50s, Commies sing
in their cells, in kitchens,
and perhaps she's old enough for kissing,
lost in pantings of arias
and imitation, but I need a car; my father's
dying and must sign for it,
how claustrophobic.

The engine's a Ford 60, '37 coupe, and a Janet
whose ring hangs from the mirror,
    but it's his hand and finger, warding off
or beckoning like the baritone Otello,
dark as that in dim lights at the drive-in,
operatic kissing of her tender lips
pushed hard into braces and the taste of blood scribbled
in his awkward signature, anonymous and carried
all the way from Winnebago:
pulses of the many engines of desire.

Hysterical chinchillas, scent of reckoning
and a sleek sister running loose
under chicken-wire cages in the blood shower:
    "Why can't we, too, be free? It's woe to the many
in maturity, scorch of the green adolescent"
sung in the dissonant imitation of a hound
under humming, my grandmother,
my jovial aunt, cake, but a pie baked

for my 58th birthday,
a long way from Winnebago, in memory's
machinery, lemon, and the sight
      of scorched meringue, as José and I
blow out the candles, wishing—
my silent interlocutor.

Chinchilla skinned to rat tail in the Windy City
worn by Wanda
at the Edgewater, eating lemon pie,
      meringue, and honey Robert
grinning over the peaks.

Janet needs a roadster "with a rumble seat!";
goodbye, then, to Chicago and ironing
to look good in the '30s,
      uncertain kisses, sleek sisters;
she has legs,
that wraparound and a pageboy,
      turning in heels at the Edgewater:
on the road again,
top down, heading toward Winnebago.

Crush of years telescoped to heat,
cake candles, McCarthy, and the machinery
      of a car born from a dead father's signature
in claustrophobic mountains of coffee cake and meringue.
It's all risen in romance, José,
      and chinchillas. Wanda has one.
Goodbye, *amante*, shuffling to the border.

Scorch in piston rings of the hot 60.
Janet's in adolescent barking
in the '30s, a roadster,
and I'm following, a fork full of meringue.

It's Winnebago once again, and Wanda
in her stolen dresses,
                hushed snare under brushes,
that lakeside parking lot, those lanterns,
The Four Freshmen and Neal Hefti.

Then it's Wanda, gazing into lust
and the skull face of the future, in chinchilla,
         there at the car window,
a long way from Chicago, mariachi music, and El Paso.

## 5. A Few Dozen People

O little town. This isn't Bethlehem,
but Congress Park. Nobody lives here anymore
that was a relative of mine.

Still it looks like a hard-working town,
one of the many wasted ones
we've traveled through

and know too of the women of this town,
your mother and the rest,
a few dozen people in the stories you told.

Hollow tones ring in the churchyard,
the bells at Senlis,
where women wear silver bells as tassels,

a little town, closer to Bethlehem, in a dream.
I'm not a traveling man, and the tassels
may be only a faint ringing in my ears,

or the metal decoration on that skirt in Scotland,
a woman catching fire in hot reflection
of a recent heat wave in the news.

Before the war, in Congress Park, there was a crèche,
in Britain a day nursery, from Old French:
Senlis and those bells.

I find cravat and cowl, under the C of Congress,
monks and dandies, and my collie,
Lady, Elizabeth, later than your stories.

What can be our covenant, the old cowcatcher
on the distant train, that haunted whistle
in the night of everyone's memories?

A decorated Bethlehem,
pots pounded in the park at war's end,
your sisters in that necessary fire of adolescence,

just a few dozen people,
and the boulder in the lawn you hopped down from
and did it once again, just as childlike at eighty.

It strikes me that I'm older than you are
in maturity, mother, youngest daughter,
though I blush now in the arrogance of that thought.

The bells were ringing in the churchyard at Senlis,
elegant Frenchmen in cravats, and the monks hid their faces
from the women under cowls. So close to Paris,

one might wonder at such innocence. But the fold
of the bells' peals, and only one of a few dozen people
paused in innocence to listen, in a dream.

It was I, mother, those bells. Can't you understand
a son borne into searching for a magic town, the congress
of a Bethlehem behind me? Close to sixty now,

and still I come to watch the house,
sisters in their adolescence spilling out,
your stem mother, and that rock of remembrance.

A woman catches fire in Scotland, metal tassels
fashioned for dancing. I imagine she does dance,
out of the fire on her way to Bethlehem.

Or maybe she's consumed by it. Or did her rough hands
pat her skirt and put it out? More likely.
Dreams exaggerate, like argument

so clotted there's no room for measure
of the real, that which never comes in reason
but in talk only, hard earned. And one must

approach carefully, often dancing.
And so the bells at Senlis, Bethlehem, your sisters,
and the places we've been and may still be going.

You're leaving, mother. It's you, but not me.
Goodbye. All this has been preparatory
to this: a story not of Bethlehem but another awkwardness.

Wanda drinks her liquor at the lake, a speak-easy
inhabited by Janet and the rest,
just a few dozen women on the brink of anger

in repose; they await the dancing, speak of make-up
and clothing, Robert and the other men.
Dogs sniff along the dark shore, nobody's pets.

The scene's set for strife and relationship,
shoplifting, and the bitching one has come to expect
from women deep in gossip in such lazy summers

in the early '30s. But a sudden storm, dogs
with their tails down, women rising to close
shutters, and before long it's laughter and forgetting

of clothing, the necessary numb of liquor,
dance parties and men. A simple story,
but I needed to say it

before the storm cleared
and Wanda and Janet put their party faces on
and went out for their engagements.

How perfectly lovely you must have been
back then. And there you are again, mother,
after all, still living,

as are a few dozen people of our acquaintance
though composition keeps changing, better rotating,
figures standing on a slowly turning diorama, a profile

then another fading into background of memory, the term
in every story of the small historical and its swelling
to meet the larger, pathetic one…

"I was alone in the desert, changing a diaper…
Once I was headed for Tucson… a trip on a Sinclair tanker
to Venezuela… Joshua panicles, passing a car's window."

I like the former better. I mean the living, mother.
Do you know what I mean? This is it,
and not for lack of complexity of thought either.

Hating Wanda in a life made of Catholicism,
disapproving of Janet,
you were in love with Robert, all of them.

Not that a man should be a son or a sweet father,
it was your sisters spilling into adolescence
ahead of you and your dead father.

It could have been that woman dancing in fire
in Scotland, her metal tassels, your mother disapproving
of that and most everything. Simplicity

of the glib psychological, a news story, bells ringing
in romance in a French Catholic village,
your son roaming in awareness of unsettledness,

and Wanda with clothes under her wedding dress,
ready, too, for travel. What can I do,
mother? I hear the train's whistle

here in my crib. It's the one
pushing the cowcatcher over the moonlit rails.
Dogs bark in this deserted night, and a cow jumps

over the moon on my wall in this little town.
I could have been dreaming of Wanda, Janet and you,
speaking easy, steaming toward Bethlehem or Senlis.


## 6. Wanda and I

Desirous of a month of Sundays,
that kind of love
       where slack spirits live

in villages like sleepy border towns
each one wayward of memory.

Upwind from the smell of camphor
and stertorous breathing—Nogales, I guess,
or El Paso—and the dogs dragging
the worried carcass,
pebbles turning in darkness in the Rio Grande.

Under the shadows of buildings, the land
leaks out to oasis,
        green groves of pecan trees,
golf courses in Nogales. What else
but the vaguest of sadness in forgetting?

Yet the music's Four Freshmen,
not these border polkas
drifting downwind from Juarez. Specifics
of a different care
with harmony, and she remembers

dancing and the economy
of sex taken in the back seat with Robert,
Neal Hefti, a variety of sidemen
and the story of a fleeing Actaeon
though her name's only Wanda.

Dogs drag the carcass and it's Lake Winnebago,
promiscuous Janet once again and summer,
one of those lakeside breezes,
boats lifting white sails red in the sunset
and El Paso a name only in the exotic.

The paso doble, the stunned finch hitting
the window glass mistaken for the air,

doweling in the headboard of the mission bed
fingered in half-sleep, my crib, Andy Panda,
Wanda and I: this fatuous music.

Faint thunder of ice cracking through a winter lake
in Wisconsin, sun cold and my brother,
our heads close together, haunted light
in the fishing hole. We speak of our mother,
forgiving each other. Wanda

is losing her mind, carapace of her husband
dragged by dogs in the dust of El Paso,
Naco, where I danced the paso doble shuffling
to border polkas, awkward
mariachis in white suits and disdain.

Or was it divorce in Nogales, the bar crowded
with those wishing for a last adultery,
      kissing of Mexican gigolos for service?
Wanda gets nervous in her story, young stag
clicking through lakeside pebbles in memory.

Hounds at our heels, inadvertent observation,
trembling of a weed and white skin, that
      face a skull turned into light
caught at her bathing, intractable rage
of any woman, even Wanda seeing Janet

in the back seat with Robert, distant tunes,
and thus they are married and he's a carapace
in the dust of El Paso, dragged by dogs.
I see a moth in the sun flattened in the crease
where the door closes, going in for coffee.

Each love is loss and remembrance. Nogales
    freezes in the winter, thunder
of my brother firing a handgun. I'd turn the barrel
to my lips, like Wanda, let love be a carapace,
return to the touch of crib doweling and mother.

And yet it's summer, the paso doble, Actaeon
turning away. Chickadees in their black
and white suits, mariachis at the border
of invisible glass and the stunned finch watched
for its life. What can I, Wanda, imagine

of your memory, my own,
or Janet in a similar room in Nogales?
She looks out a window as we do,
golfers or your green groves of pecan trees,
or my own sea, blue between pine limbs at horizon.

Derelict, as a finch fallen to thistle, that crib
and the signature of new teeth on a rattle,
my little velvet suit: these common losses.
The lovers awaken, stunned still in the dream
of dogs dragging a carcass, the finch shudders

in the anonymity of its nature, before my eyes.
All rise. Lake Winnebago, the shimmer of Wanda's
white dress passing the dew-laden fenders,
paper lanterns, looking for Janet, distant harmony,
Four Freshmen, the last song, my Neal Hefti.

What else but a skull turned in the moonlight
in the window and her perfect legs? It's Janet
she should have married, seeing the shuffling
carapace at the periphery over the sill:
El Paso, the paso doble, stertorous breathing.

I am not Robert. Lusting for Janet, old bones
shift south toward the border, thoughts of a few
sidemen lifting, like instruments,
her white body as my Four Freshmen deliver
loss always, nostalgia, and Wanda weeps

for the lost opportunity. It's always that,
not memory of thunder's echo through ice,
fingers in the doweling of the mission crib,
Andy Panda, Lake Winnebago
remaining a name only in the exotic.

Stale coffee and our cups cold on the sills.
Janet looks through the clear glass at Nogales,
thinking of Robert. Wanda, still weeping,
thinks of her. One of us is losing our mind
in the paso doble, signature of new teeth

on a rattle. Mother. The stunned finch rises ancient,
though a fledgling in the summer air.
The lovers awaken to the mariachis, Janet,
Wanda and I, and the dogs drag the worried
carcass, a carapace, across the border.

## Typical Sad Song

I can imagine that long winter in Provincetown,
fog, and a sky of pitted slate
on days you called clear.

Her siren song arrived in rusty voice,
holding you there, from the peninsula.

I can imagine you by smoky hearth light,
in that party dress,
drinking medicinal toddy.

How pandemic was your days' damp accomplishment,
that cancerous dyspepsia.
Even the crabs'
shuttle on the flats seemed drunken from Angelica.

We could have been elsewhere, you and I,
but for crazy love and bartenders.
Thus, when she returned again you had rotted.

Now a summer breeze blows out the fog and dampness,
dries away mildew, but for tourists.
Only I remain to ride her siren song again to lust.

She has money, a Florida sun tan, festival promises,
and you are six feet down,
looking into a typical slate sky in Provincetown.

## The Sign

What I needed to do
        was find and read some book that comes
with a sign. But it was *Sapolin*,
this time
        unenameled by Duchamp,
set askew
on broken wooden sleds
        beside a (barber's) pole in air,
androgynous silk sweaters,
and a creel hung at the mouth
        of this seductive little place
dressed up to look
like a swap-shop.

Janet's
up ahead already,
talking to the woman inside, remarks
        on the oddness of furniture
and faked jewels
and on her bruised arm:
        that rheumatoid arthritis— "It's
the medication,
any,
friendly, little bump."—

        and you've gone,
to journey
down the crowded aisles in china,
hanging
        gardens of lamps, curious
in curios,
just looking around.

I trip the bell at the door, thinking
of ice fishing,
and that man
        in a silk sweater, on a sled,
riding
into a mountain town, somewhere,
for a hair cut:
        it's the start
of a story
I'm constructing from these objects, this place,
        seen, and then imagined—
smell of talcum and rum,
        the lovers' seductive disguise.
In the snow
a car idles at the curb
as the plot thickens.

Outside,
there's a sudden spring storm
        to surprise us in our leaving,
something in the air.
It's petunias,
in planters at the fence
bruised by the rain, releasing
their scent
as if in defense against some enemy,
        stunning that life-giving friend,
intimately, with perfume!

This, then is the sign.
        The one I bought reads *Sapolin*,
letters beaded by rain,
        as if somebody's tears in the story,
frozen in deceit, passion, or death,
face up in the trunk.

## Hat in Hand

The captain stood in the narrow passage,
gold braid at the shoulder,
slightly rocking, hat in hand.
Inside,
      beyond the elegant cabin hatch: two women,
one sure of herself,
attractive in that sternness, a little manly,
the other awkward and hesitant, yet beautiful.

No matter the century, the names, or the story,
or if the ship, bound for Java, carries coal.
No matter that all the stories have been told
and are told yet again.

Two women,
a ship bound for Java, and the kind of gesture
that is a presage of the official or of courtship.

Could be the vessel is fitted out in memory,
and whose hand now is at the wheel?
No matter that the hatch opens on a bloody chamber.

The ship is bound for Java; perhaps it carries coal.
It rides low in the water
seen from the sea.

## Human Nature

I remember angelic voices
and seeing them,
      shadow figures
of nuns'
hats in the choir loft,
against a paradise fresco.

Somewhere
      in Switzerland,
this time of year,
          grain scent in manure,
and bells to announce
their singing,
      where we stood
in the courtyard waiting
and virginal.

At least on this
          first summer day, the cats
have quit that sexual crying,
stunned by the burgeoning,
though robins
      celebrate their nests
incessantly. Loss,

and then again that German boy
in his lederhosen,
      the way her voice rose
into the spiritual,
a long time ago,
          as will the kingdom come
out of the past.

Misuse
of what I have so recently
come to appreciate, your lip
        lifted in that smile,
cherries may be
                the best fruit,
the flow of oil in the white stain.

But recently the clouds have come in
        bitter, out of the northeast, low
from the sea. Those stranded
                in the campground
have reminded me of accident
in time's seasonal rotation,
                just a week's vacation,
charcoal
rain-soaked and useless.

Company
of a dozen or so sisters,
        a caravan for light,
her voice rising in that shadow choir,
believing
        in just about anything.
Although the fresco's only
                a painting of paradise,
those figures,
leaning in expectancy,
cleansed even of sex now.

Yet a caravan,
        broken in accident at a border town,
you in the company
of Clair and Dot in London.

Imagining something
in the shadow background in that fresco,
maybe a common camper, an Airstream,
and the story of a dozen people
traveling,
       hats off in the sun,
and conversation
touched by the pleasures of intrigue,
eyes' false betrayal absent,
       squinting in a small Cape Cod
village at a house sale.
       It's home,
where the singer comes to appreciate
her furniture in the yard, that cutlery,
some sort of science fiction
dead end.

The caroling of the wind is lost to itself
as in all failed resolve.
I sip the coffee.
       Pages turn,
and the wind crumbles, reaching gorse
at the lowlands,
where reeds shake, anchored
       in the tide marsh, holding it for a moment
before swallowing.
The pages settled down along the spine,
       now, as always, just
a little too late.
       "I don't know nothing,"
he'd said, lying
       in his teeth again,
that habit,
and scent of dead fish in the estuary
he'd been poaching,

    then came on dreams of her silken hair,
abandoned garments,
      luridly snaked in the reeds'
forest of the new world.

This was our home, and still
   is spoken of often,
a lost profile
of middens and corn farms.
He'd taken her purchase order on the rubber raft,
   the counter between them as wide
as the continental shelf.
Angelic, even in high school,
    she'd looked up only
to discover
their past momentarily blinking. "Nothing,
   I don't know nothing
about it."

Or about that elevated place, our thighs
pressed against saddles
   riding up to the crest
on mavericks,
half broken
     and still bewildered
from dark transit
   up from the south, two abreast
in horse trailers
    rocking at worn hitches
on the rough highway.

Was it palomino? certainly
   that color, and later
Calvin enraged
not for the horse but the damaged saddle.

Kids, and not cowboys,
        rolled on the ground laughing
in our dusty hats.

This was our home,
        coils of garter snakes under the steps,
blessed relief
in some long historical romance:
diamonds, from charcoal in the crucible,
to be sold for gold?

…and came to a place where people
        of old age
                seemed my contemporaries.
The flattery was excruciating.
        But to pillory the aged
was not, then, my intention.
                I had the papers in my pocket
Some inside were women.
I'd recognized the name over the door.

Careless Love.

The hammer comes down hard in the dream,
a ball-peen missing the thumb.
        I've come, then, to appreciate
accident,
a veil blown across
a regretful face, your hair
curled in water at the drain recently.
                Something about motion and gravity,
the flow of oil in the white stain,
that ladder
leaned at the house side, expectantly.

But caravans in a new light after all
at the campground,
   clicks of crockery and utensils,
and voices risen
not in song of some paradise, but this place,
   singing the good news
of bluefish, in shore, on the backside
and charcoal drying in the sun.

This was our home
   and still remains
painfully angelic,
noble in memory's arrogance.
Yet, of things soon forgotten,
   "I don't know nothing,"
but dreams of somebody's silken hair,
snaked in the reeds' forest
of the new world.

"How is it I have found my way
to Switzerland?"
We drove up into the mountains
then, above Luzern, and saw the *Alpenglühen*.

It's evening. Miracle
   of the new moon's
a clock again. It's summer,
and robins cry incessantly, nest building.
What is required?
   Dark clouds
form caravans
at horizon, then night comes,
those other birds, and the clouds crumble.

Maybe it's this constancy of the virginal
in our attentions, placid,
and without effort and without thought.
I remember angelic voices,
        but it was only
a radio. Something passes in moonlight
in the living room:
the shadow of your smile.

# DARKLIGHT

## Darklight

Darklight above the doorway
in both X-ray and photography . . .

but not the deep significance this time
or the surface

which vibrates in the eternal present.
It's the way of the world seen

and the one apprehended, blue moon
in a haze of yellow

[she was older than she was in reality,
the fire in the hearth had died away]

though on some days
there's a certain clarity of light.

I fear this kind of thing increases
as time goes by,

though it's not exactly like that,
maybe sad sack's meanderings, half blind.

And I think this means the end is coming
before too long. If it is possible

I will miss you. In the meantime
perhaps this undeveloped deep

in dated chemical's reaction
can rise to the surface

and also be interesting,
as delicate and sentimental.

I could ride forth on a pale horse
called Dark Lantern

whose light can be blocked off
as by a sliding panel.

## Hesitation Waltz

Returned again to find that spot
    where I had rested. It was gone
or changed utterly, so that I could not sit
as pivot for consideration
        nor find comfort in standing
above the spot.

All this had been mine: window, table
and chair, that illusion
    of a virgin's intensity in seeing
each beloved distinctly,
the objective world.

A tube driven into a congested throat,
    the withdrawal of a cannula
for breathing, that moment,
then a jay's cry
    called song
which is made light of in poetry,
but is lighter than that.

*Here's that rainy day,*
    its first word, "maybe,"
held in Bill Evans' fingers for exhaustion
of what might have been,
or a big band rendering
of *Sentimental Journey,*
a medley,
*blame it on my youth,* so
*sweet and lovely.*

Once came to a place heady
with possibilities of tempo,

was crazy for intricate figures
in the cowboy squares.
        That was dancing, fleetingly,
like the memory
of freestyle later,
    an Arizona stumblebum.
What is revealed, but such hesitations
as we go down?

Yet it's still early May, clatter
    of wet chickadees insistent
pin points of black-cap on the pine's needles
        (be then
joyful?),
dissonant melodies over block chords,
a red sail in the damp distance,
    considerations of tables and chairs.
*I can't get started.*

Rivers of memory, sea of memory, rainy ripples
    on a golden pond, notoriously placid
and temporary, before the arrival
        of the actors
and strife.
It's come from the desert of my boyhood
in some fashion. That boat.

    These are the pines grown into a screen
at the pond's brink.
        This is automatic writing.
The trees cry out
as the axe enters the forest,
    "Look at the handle,
he's one of us!"
I could have discovered

that note thrown on the kitchen table,
but for the boy
        wobbly now at the gunnels
near the axe handle tiller;
he's fighting
the red sail and adolescence.
    "I'm leaving": her words
fluttering to linoleum in a household breeze.
I can see them,
in the mind's eye, through the window.

Once came in dreaming to the pond's brink.
    Once saw a girl's undergarments
in her spinning in a cowboy square.
        I was hesitant: *blame it on my youth*.
The pond was placid
in a river cast down by the moon.
    I could see the red sail, that bloody rag
of adolescence.

Watching a girl's undergarments in the mind's eye,
        no more than a stable speck in this imagination.
Yet it's still early May.
Dissonant candles
    shake like awkward dancers
in the cowboy squares,
        my sentimental journey.
I should light them at the tips
as we go down
into a moon river at this window.

Repeated figures of the dance, actual
    in the memory: cowboys looping
near a flash of undergarments
        below crinoline,

notes spilling
to a wash of sawdust near a household table,
"I'm leaving,"
gone into the death that is memory
        of a boy's boat under red sail
at the pond's iris, her face
        then rising like the moon itself
through seaweed.

This is the danger zone of the virgin.
This is automatic writing.
        These are the spot's projections
on the pond's moonglow surface,
        a carousel of shadowy faces,
my dream girls, under glass.

Yet in this rain, old interlude, other
seeds germinate invisibly
        in that sodden garden, awaiting
the new chicken-wire fence
and rabbits, some wholesomeness
of hard work
        beyond thoughts of dream girls
as women,
        or a few popular tunes: *slowpoke,*
*heart of my heart, red roses*
*for a blue lady,*
        hesitant *deep purple*
in a cowboy waltz tempo.

The cardinals have arrived,
        their insouciant arrogance tentative
in first flowers wavering
        on delicate green stalks, daffodils
heavy in a freight of rain, goldfinch,

red red robin,
a mix of wild bird seed in the rickety feeders,
   that geometric pattern
of quick chickadees lifting
      some invisible net of crinoline,
gold spun, and the weaving traces
of my neighbor's
black cat through hay.

It's early May too in that distant desert:
   what buds, what boy? Each memory
only a fake of hesitant music,
be it squares
   or the bright blindness of *moonglow*.
This is automatic writing,
   "as the axe enters the forest."
Try to forget it, in this
burgeoning.

   But we were dancing, or she was
spinning alone on her own spot, elsewhere
      and ecstatic,
within that isolate figure,
one of many,
characteristic of a cowboy square,
   unaware of those spectator figures,
      to the far corners of the hall
and the one rocking us gently,
   that childish wrangler and his allemande girl,
the hum of the world turning
under the sawing fiddles and guitars.

We fumbled around in our bodies,
   got crazy over supposed slights
and adulteries.

        We went to the movies
for those common agonies,
        traded a few awkward kisses
            in a dark alcove in Tucson
that time we drove there for a school concert
in your mother's car.
Even then,
given such virginal passions,
this was not exactly clear.

I remember the ice-cream cones,
        at Castle Rock below Copper Man.
It was early spring
and sundown:
        your eyes, your face!
We licked our chops,
at the taste. *That* was sweet.

There was even a boat with a red sail,
        a boy in shadow at the tiller
on a pond in desert oasis,
Saint David,
        not exactly golden
but still water
fed from a deep wellspring, no pines,
but willows at the brink.

        "I'm leaving," going off to Texas
for another teen life.
        The tiller wobbles
under his hand in a quick breeze.
Enter the axe.

*I'm through with love*
        (for a little while
at least).

All this is part
of the disposition of the figures in the dance,
    though they are not actors,
so long as acts of memory
        are discounted,
as well as an old man's garrulous
enthusiasms
in searching elsewhere for his spot.

    Beyond the window now,
in fog and rain,
the sun sets this evening like clockwork,
a common perception
recently.

    And if the world doesn't hum
in its turning, I seem to
and imagine
that pine, skeletal
        in slow advancing,
as it fades back into shadow
and the axe flashes
        at the pond's brink. Here it comes.
It is one of us.

## Swiss Miss

Lingers now in peace upon the swollen tide,
ruby-throat fallen from sky in the last few hours.
This information: unblemished, on her good side,
not sleeping, and Swiss birds won't eat thistle.

After the circus and before investigation,
the fliers linger on imagination, the Bohemian
Waxwing juggler, those quick Chickadee tumblers.
The Swiss detective wears wingtips.

Lisalot, I miss you, I didn't mean to release you.
Flights of fancy and flocking in the banquet hall,
while the river, beyond filmy curtains and balcony,
runs to the lake, carrying her body as if sleeping.

Ladies and gentlemen, if you will please quit chattering,
if you will just try hard to remember, the details,
anything in the recent past. It shouldn't be difficult.
Time was I loved you, dear Lisalot, I never dropped you.

Check everyone's wrists, the nature of their shoes and
identification. Is there residual powder in anyone's palms?
Check times of arrival, those missing, each performer.
Remember, Swiss birds won't eat thistle.

Was it the proud German, Finch? That week in Luzern?
You flew as a hummingbird from the bar then, in Bern.
And check also the Limmat River, send in the clowns.
Embraceable you, sweet ruby-throat, I've washed my hands.

Feathered boas and short tights in the banquet hall,
Madam Vireo, the contortionist, and her dwarf entourage.
Check for splinters, look most carefully under the nails.
Lisalot: tossed high up in the contest in St. Gallen.

We were the rage of the competition, the odd birds
who flew out in our nature and faked danger theatrically
after those months of practice, home in Furna. I never
looked at you closely, gripping your ankles, in that way.

Then the German, Finch. Or was it that Harlequin, Jaeger?
Take but a moment to consider, Swiss birds won't eat thistle,
then take each one into a room, backstage, and ask questions.
Lisalot, my darling partner, little Swiss Miss, I warned you.

[General atmosphere: the river, ominous mist over the lake,
the Swiss detective, maybe elaborate cages hung in the hall.
He could be innocent, an accident. She could be a strumpet.
His hands, or he stands at the rear of the line murmuring.]

Please stop chattering. Defend your heads against the cages.
Prepare, please, your stage and real names and associations.
Have you been with the circus long? How well did you know
Lisalot? Things like that. What can you tell me about thistle?

Then, in Grindelwald, we were eager. The Eiger rose majestic
above the chalet, your hair silk feathers in my fingers.
Lisalot, you called my nose a beak, humming softly in laughter.
Almost love birds in an alpine cage! What becomes of me now?

A dwarf stands upon the shoulders of the Strong Man, Hawk.
His real name is Meadowlark and it's taking far too long.
He opens a few cages. Pandemonium! The fledglings can't
fly well, and feathers and death squawks flood the Hall.

[I too have been crazy in jealousy. Our cat, Flicker,
and the foreign sock he discovered under our bed.
I wanted to kill you, quite seriously, or myself then.
You, strumpet; I the virtuous dove, already in mourning.]

Attention, please. Attention! Can you please settle down?
Lunch is on the way. We'll be serving thistle today . . .
That's right, it's a joke. It's seed salad, and flesh
for those inclined. Thank you for your attention anyway.

Lisalot, Finch or Jaeger, it doesn't matter; even exotic
Bachman, warbling MC, whose song might have seduced you.
Just as I was beginning to touch you, take you under my wing.
Better had you avoided hunger, throat swelling with thistle.

Be sure, now, to check the empty cages, secreted places,
keep an eye on the ground feeders, as well as flycatchers.
Close all the windows. The ones under suspicion might
seem without guile. Clearly, this was a crime of passion.

Thistle: in his pockets, in his cuffs, in his hair; also
there is thistle in the matting over muscle on his arms.
I smell thistle! It's our detective, perky as a sparrow.
Thistle's stuck in ducts, visible at the corners of his eyes.

[I too have wept around thorns, stuck in rageful weeping.
Somehow love is indecent, if ethical considerations apply.
Yet the moves of your glorious legs. I can't describe them,
but in metaphor: legs of a hawk hanging down at landing.]

Okay, I killed you, thistle in the muesli. I'm sorry.
The last thing I wanted to do, etcetera. It was a mistake,
but I am not innocent. Lisalot, even if a dozen young men
had slept with you, even then I would still love you.

From the dead: Fuck you! I was no willing object of such
sentimental crap. I had my own agenda, and you killed me.
Christ, is it gentle here on the waves, almost exquisite,
to sleep deep on my side upon water, no man beside me.

Please behave yourselves. Miss Pelican, stop with the soaring.
The line grows shorter, and I grow increasingly satisfied.
Miss Pelican! It's a long way yet to Tipperary, but one bird
ate thistle, and thistle hangs around. Miss Swan, that's enough!

Lisalot! Your body turning cartwheels in the air, blah, blah,
your orchestrated clothing, tights forcing men into despair.
Your hair: innocent as chick-down or a diaper, blah, blah.
What can I say now? I still love you. I offer the proof.

[Your orchestrated clothing to say, I am here, look at me.
Perhaps love of necessity contains jealousy. I told you to go,
go, get out of here, only because you slept with another.
This is not love, but hypocrisy. Let me die in your arms.]

Difficulties among flycatchers, high wire and trapeze.
Count Scissortail comes to blows with a certain Phoebe,
a ruckus about relatives and partners. Madam Vireo is miffed,
sends out her dwarfs. The detective calls once again for order.

Quick as water up from the well in Furna, my sister,
news of incest on the high wire throughout the village.
It never happened. Check the quieter Towhees, their feathers.
Lisalot, each gesture, each flight, each time I caught you.

[Atmosphere: the hall a complete mess, feathers and blood,
empty as this apartment, the fled nest, no Lisalot, no you.
Thistle weighs him down, a loadstone, as much as absence
pricks like needles in our pillows, my clothing, this chair.]

You're next, last in line. Raise your arms. Wait! Where
are you going? Come back! Check the curtains, the balcony!
[Beware of extremity, hopeless desperation, and suicide.]
Then check the river for her brother, Pigeon, no kingfisher.

# Dream

Dreamed of a woman lonely in a country house,
a married woman, younger than I,
with no children. It was not her dream,
though she was standing at a window
romantically in yearning. There was faint light
on a table, her form provocative in shadow.

Perhaps she was waiting for her husband
instead of me. It doesn't matter, for it was not
his dream, though he might have been thinking
carefully about her. Not really a dream,
rather a thought provoking nightmare,
since she was lonely and I was not yet there.

Dreams that are manageable, like this one,
are not dreams at all. One thinks of glory,
the passions of a savior, complete control.
She was waiting for someone approaching
on a white horse? in a cab? after a spring rain,
cuffs dampened, unruly hair, that kind of thing.

Perhaps dreaming, her eyes pass over the porch,
alight on the circular wishing-well in the garden
her husband has carefully tended, wending his way
among tender shoots, thinking of children.
Birds call. Little spring rabbits appear.
I have the answer, the key, the disruptive solution.

There is time now for the sun and the music,
for fairy-tale children dancing around the well.
There might have been time for his returning,
but this is nightmare, clouds come in, and it begins

to rain again. I might have been out there, hesitant,
under the wet young leaves of the tender oaks.

Time enough for dreaming, a dream that is not one.
Has she taken a tranquilizer, to wend herself away
from barrenness? There is time left for wishing,
but the well is a fake one, cheap, and poorly assembled.
Her husband spends time in a bar among lascivious women.
I am not sure if I am him or the fairy-tale children.

## Calaca

Mystery of the unlikely, a ghost story,
but this is after the tale
    began in death and decay,
but not death,
for peonies grew from the skull's eyes,
defying that gravity
        where flesh fell, after it had risen
back to the earth's surface in hurricane,
that clear spring afternoon
    when he had leaned down
over bone, the universal visage now.
Alas, poor Madeline!

[The nose grows larger, relative
to weight loss and the shrinking flesh,
then lastly
    the nose itself falls away,
no more to be lifted
in gesture of offence taken
        nor flared out at the nostrils
in the throes of passion. 'Throes"?
    I was almost gone away
at those times,
throwing myself away.]

Before the hurricane, back pedaling, before
offense taken
    as the doctor inserted the cannula,
before these material changes
       it seemed better
to move on the earth politically,
    though eventually caught that way

in criminal secrets revealed
to the far corners of the village.

[And the teeth!
What burdens are set aside
when hair falls down at the crown?
    Living by the skin of them, a skull fracture
knocking some sense in.
        To be excused,
to run on counter to expressed wishes.
I was full of myself
    those times, myself
not full of me.]

Before the reversal of fortune and the hurricane,
before night was day and Madeline the calaca,
    before light in the head lamp of the doctor,
all seemed well in the seaside village,
their serious lives,
    that comedy of complete wastefulness
celebrated.

Madeline:
cooking and cleaning, sewing,
    shopping for dinner and his comfort,
doing a little ironing, at mid-day
in the kitchen,
a focus of soreness below the clavicle.

He brought in money
and a certain perfected oblivion.
She was a dancer
    for joy and not money,
in a previous life clearly remembered.
A bell played at the gate

upon his arrival, each evening,
before day was night
    and the doctor,
there
in the throes of political passion
and the sweet presences
of the here and now.

[Brewed cups of eroded memory,
    cauldron of the catalytic world. I drink
from a dipper,
flesh hangs down in the gravity,
    and the feet! and the grinding ratchet
in the shoulder!
        Were it your slipper, young
and vibrant before hurricane.
The hair falls out at the crown.]

Before the hurricane and the buildings toppled,
the madonna Madeline sits at the window
    a vision of satisfaction
when looking in.
Looking out, there's a vibrant commerce,
    the real world.
A bell plays at the gate.
She's fallen dead at the window,
just sixty-two.

[Yesterday,
stupidity of lost opportunity.
    The flesh hangs slack at the throat,
a groaning when turning
in the empty bed. And the knees,
        filaments clouding the right eye.
Who is the one left to be following?

Drink deep from the dipper.
    Mystery of the unlikely, a ghost story.
Were it your slipper.]

Posada rendered the personalities of the calaveras,
    and this is becoming a village full of them,
skeletons in the streets and parks,
a number present, always, at public gatherings
and the ones arriving by boat, caught up
    in hurricane and shipwreck,
who now build a bonfire on the beach
for singing, eating, and dancing
below the rocky cliffs.

He was a politician, caught out for vote selling.
Poor Madeline. He can see her
    through the window now,
the calaca,
that parody of himself reclaiming
his reputation and stature.
    She's calling out to the gathering
wearing his clothing,
suit, *sombrero* and tie.
    Symbols of words vomit in the bone faces
of the calaveras, her jaw clacking
to convince the populace.

    And the story might end here, a lesson,
but you know, he too the skeleton
    after hurricane and resurrection
and the dancer, Madeline
assuming that ethical self he had forgotten
even in sustenance from the dipper.
He fell down dead at the window.

[Yet I am still in love!]

He, now, the calaca,
cooking and cleaning, wearing a dress
and her slippers,
waiting for bells at the gate,
but in a parody of waiting for domesticity
    possible only in gestures
        of the unexpressive skull.
Though criminal,
    yet he is at peace and happy,
if such can be said of calacas,
here in a paradise
paid for in lost stature
in the other.
        He's sitting at the window, sewing,
while outside the skeletons are dancing.

Paradise,
the seating of company
    and the defying of gravity,
the teeth recessional again
and the nose in place:
    all burdens are set aside, feet
shoulder and knees.
Here, then
    the products of shipwreck,
a bottle,
a hairpiece and sour lemons,
    dead fish in the water,
a chicken,
and the survivors
    come from the sea resurrected
as calaveras.

[I could put the pot on the table, the dipper,
arrange the silver and napkins,
supply the salt cellar.
        Stupidity of lost opportunity,
the *mariachis* are playing again
and I can't be there.
        Stupidity at public gatherings,
lies and deception.
I could shrink down into these bones, under
this flimsy clothing.
        I think I'll do that.
No more stories to tell.
The hair fallen out at the crown.]


…this fire, this chicken, this story, these
*mariachis* and survivors dancing,
        smell of dead fish and whispers
of jetsam from shipwreck in this quiet sea.
This good fellowship
and the presence of women in this telling.
        Pass over the bottle now and the lemon.
Calaca, pinch me a pinch of salt.
We have nowhere to get to, nothing to do.
And this is paradise.

## Prayer of Initiation

I pray upon entrance
into the Brotherhood of Endings.
I've given up my feet as offering
to the end of walking around.
      Soon enough, forgetfulness,
first marker of stupor,
confusing machines
and the clicking of various appliances
misunderstood as voices.
      Dear Brotherhood,
that Sisterhood might tend me
even in anger at my early leaving,
even in disgust,
that phrases in our rambling conversations
act as germination of wisdom's ideas
for somebody's children.
      After decline into no stamp collecting
or gardening, into nothing recognizable
as work or even significant
statement to turn heads momentarily,
after lyrics and fingers
losing their way in mud shuffles
among keys and strings, what then
but this Brotherhood, this prayer of endings?
      I went south to Galveston.
I thought upon the shark constantly moving
and the brothers behind curtains in old houses.
I went east to New Bedford
and thought there upon the vegetables
I once tended, a garden gone now
to seed and new growth
of weeds, wild and apprehensive
in their disorderly beginnings.

The possible became dreaming in waking,
the acutely intimate the distances
at the outward signs.
All the sisters, in triage
have traveled away elsewhere
to tend others. Where now are my brothers?
I cannot see or hear them
and have forgotten
all these beginnings before the end.

## Accident of the Axe

As perhaps you have recently noted, given
the cooler, the steel head, and the ankle,
there was considerable pain immediately after

though very little in the way of blood.
I sat down on the stump itself, alone
but for my wife

who was off somewhere picking berries.
Certainly, I was responsible, and there in the ice
in deep throbbing, I thought about this:

no fault of the axe, tree, or the sunlight.
And I thought about walking out
into the sunlight, coming forth

from under the shadows of branches.
In this morning of a new day,
I could walk all the way to Stockholm,

at least to Cairo, Illinois, the nearest big town.
In Cairo was a Swedish woman I was fooling with then
who lived in a white house with four children,

a house my wife had driven by slowly.
I know this because the woman had seen her
and the jig was up, temporarily.

But recently we had started up again,
and I was thinking of the playset in her front yard,
hopping around on the lawn with her children.

Perhaps the look of her was in my eyes,
or it was my own look as I came into her in memory,
melted away with her. I can't be sure,

but I was ready to walk all the way to Cairo.
Then my wife came up to me, right into my face,
then saw the foot in the grass beside me

probably thinking at first it was some animal.
"That's your reward!" she cried out flushed in anger,
then fell down dead at the cooler.

Her berry can had strewn its contents on the ground,
a sort of red coagulant beside the foot.
I felt very much like walking away to get help.

I bought the axe near the Swedish woman's house,
my lame excuse for going over that way.
Perhaps it was barrenness that caused the fatal rage.

Never mind the axe, the shadows, or the sunlight.
Accidents happen, and it's only the insurance policy
I write about. Never mind the Swedish woman either.

This is my claim. All the premiums were paid up.
I'm on crutches and a veteran of foreign wars.
You can send the check ahead to Cairo.

## At Some Time

Are the gigolos nervous?
I can't tell.
    That one in tights
and sequins?
        It's swell
that the party went your way
at the end, though clearly every night
was a new beginning.

    Yet I was lonesome, 3 AM
and nothing to do but watch them.
Sure, I could drive you home
at first light.
What right had I to refuse
the dancing?

"You're nothing
    but a strumpet."
"And you, my dear, are nutless."
      Just driving along, typically,
before your blood on the seat.

At some time or other,
    we were, I guess, "happy
to see you. Did you sleep well?"
        Or do I imagine that you spoke
gently over breakfast.
Then somebody just appeared,
that one in sequins.

Machinery of forensics,
      as on television, your car
completely dismantled,

for blood is telltale as testament
to all-seeing detectives,
just gigolos like all the others.
You deserved it, luckily
the axe was handy.

[The body's tenderness: I'd overdriven
   those barricades,
lucky in love, then attention
at the right time.
            Axe into flesh?
The bright warning signs were yellow.
      A complete awareness of fragility
since then.
It could have been otherwise.]

Stunned, ever since then, by lack of wisdom.
The obvious escaped them.

[Obeisant to the trees
   that give us paper, housing
and shade,
the handle is wooden.
Though the blade bite deep,
         there's no bleeding
but for sap.
      The scalpel, something
else entirely, is made for flesh.
But I was put to sleeping then
and did not cry out.]

Running ever since then with gigolos,
wearing sequins
      cut away in fabric taken
from your dresses. Our eyes are upon

money, sister,
what's provided by cruel and lonely women.
    You were the one exception
at some time or another, over breakfast:
have a nice day. The way
you spoke when you weren't screaming.

[Some other accidents: pricking a finger,
    just imagine the whole hand
lopped off. Won't muscles contract,
        squeezing the arteries against
too much bleeding?
    The delicate white neck, shaving,
swell of the barked knuckle,
her fragile temple, the car seat.]

Over this time I am losing energy.
    I get sick on the off nights,
not from guilt,
        but increasing remembrances
of good times, which is loss.
Do you remember, of course you can't now,
times at the beach
    when we were younger, traveling
down Mexico way for enchiladas,
        sum sum Summertime
and those other foolish songs
from our generation?
    Look at that one, she's ready,
but I have no heart for it.
        "What kind of day did you have?"
over dinner.

[Accident of the head turning too suddenly,
something in the neck.]

That's what I said, over dinner,
and later,
    at times during the entire evening,
"What kind of day did you have?"
        "Would you like a cocktail?"
Then sleeping,
just the two of us
in sweet oblivion, together.

[Stronger than a vicious tide, able to leap
to the room's center, then call out
over the bed to the sleeping lovers:
    This Ends in Tragedy.
Yet who is that,
but indulged imagination?
    All the wounds would be real,
sharp, chopping cuts on the palms, defensive,
visible brain matter,
    like wet gobs ripped away
from a natural sponge, in her temple.]

Please indulge me. Please try to understand.
    It was the dancing, my desire
for gigolos
until I was one of them
    and with them, a breath of clean air.
It wasn't difficult to kill her,
    the axe was there, but it was
this other thing, I say love
and its attendant madness that drove me.
Beyond reason?
Can this forgive me?
    I sleep alone these days,
stay to the side when among gigolos.
I always try to dance

          with the best dancer.
She reminds me of you.

[It seems so long that I have been waiting
        for the knife, the gun, the sledge hammer
and the axe. I even anticipate the needle, my red
blood rising in the tube.
                I wait, of course, with trepidation
for the undesired.
Would a stroke be the same, a heart attack:
just a brief pain, and then nothing?
        No wonder this fascination with the implement,
strategies for putting it off.]

No statute of limitations, but time goes by.
The memory goes by, and the vessel
holding the memory, that too goes by.

[Remember, when we were children,
        I stepped on glass in the river,
or the time
I fell, and have since
named it The Broken Clavicle?
        Certainly there is pain's echo
in new pain: this is like
that time, though of this time only.
        The memory goes by, but the vessel
holding the memory
carries the evidence of it, these scars
that can ache at times.
                I call them The Statutes, meaning
position or status,
    a ruler to measure the down slope,
or possibly, when half-dreaming,
it's the canvas in which I am written.]

Of brotherhood, when they are lovers,
    and of cruel, beautiful women:
gigolos
are made for dancing, escorting,
consorting against husbands who have
    worn out their welcome.
Cavorting?
I've a vague memory of a river,
    wasn't it glass,
and your pretty foot cut in the wading?
Didn't we do something intimate after?
    I thought of it briefly
when I twisted my ankle
dancing.
    But time moves on
and I grow too old for romancing.
I've packed my bag. Farewell to women
and gigolos,
even the one in sequins,
    who started all this. Hey, José,
Bye Bye.

## Theatrical Story

Rivers can rise romantically above their banks
at flood tide, in movies; there may be women
in shifts in good shape clinging to chimneys.
They are not yet my desire.

Just as I was about to enter.
As she was leaving.
After the party but before sleeping.
Down by the riverside in moonlight.

The story grows more complex over the years,
ho hum, no others care for this drama.
I was running ahead to save her,
possibly a stitch in time. Nobody cares.

Light as a single tortilla, the damaged dancer,
south of the border, to have chased her
in the music of mariachis, tripping
under bougainvillea, down Mexico way.

And nobody cares for the politician,
his mother and father, those who were saintly
and taught him the right road: applause
from the audience, tentative. Empty orchestra.

I keep using that term. Is it empty
of singers, conductor, even the instruments?
Nobody cares for the passing years, but
for the movies, those entertainments.

Just as I was about to enter, in Mexico,
she was leaving on her crutches.
After the party but before sleeping together,
tentatively, down by the riverside in moonlight.

## Standard-16, I Remember You

Like the memory of that moody jazz
leaking out under tent flaps
    at a California pleasure fair
or pages scattered from a long forgotten book,
word fertilizer
helping flowers seed,
blossom and become vegetables for bees,
how often have I cast
    these things aside, only
to retrieve them again, transformed,
soiled and degraded?


That summer . . .
    That fall before winter avocados
fell from their brittle stems,
    ignorant of them
in our own green flush,
    what ancillary music
did we brighten our smoggy days with
against various futures and ambitions?


The thrill of it all,
    light as a feather fallen
from some passing jay,
minus that awakening call.
We were the rage
of our sixties circle, which included
only us.


I can't remember you too well,
    but like an old shoe
found deep in the dark closet,
    you left that clothing in haste,

and I was glad for it,
        your limping at Lillian Way,
half shod in the stench of eucalyptus
and grinning sheepishly.
        How romantic, these remainders:
old devil unmentionables
and deflated beach ball for devil sun.

Nothing is like anything else.
The rain falls in fog all afternoon,
        then stutters along into early evening,
when the breeze dies down
for moratorium, and the pine candles
are stiff sentinels.
        Then we have that stillness,
ladies and gentlemen, in which dead time
is for memory's reconstructions,
if only from a few fleeting details.

        It's much like the rain itself,
a little depressing,
but it helps flowers grow, even though
nothing is like anything else.

You're often the one
downstage among so many others,
        mother's wishes for a sisterhood
of like minded souls,
        a host of dead friends
and mild mannered enemies waiting
in the shadowy wings,
for a little while (a moment ago?),
        from a distance,
inaccessible

and fortified by a brew of Sangria
fashioned from local fruits.

Just lying around, just
putting our feet up on the coffee table,
      just heading out on the Triumph
for the vineyards, carefully
my dears, for I'm alone now in memory
and not saddle sore. What's more,
      there seems a dozen of you there
behind me on the buddy-seat.

From time to time
      I danced in the foyer,
sad to remember.
      I cannot speak of adult comfort,
whatever that is,
just being in one place at a time.

Like nothing else after stormy weather,
young grapes on the vine,
      the beginning of a wine fashion
in the Napa Valley;
we might have fallen
      down in the vineyard itself
to watch them grow,
though Gallo in a jug those days for us,
      the start of darker days
of no common sense at all:
      married in the name only
of love and not money
or any comparable maturity,
light as a fallen feather, glandular.

A strumpet?
Chet Baker's voice and trumpet? Those angles
of repose along the river bed
        in the town of El Monte
when I was much younger,
before that wisdom I still don't have.
        Embraceable you or any other
was quite enough.

Mother?,
no psychology of that kind,
        yet family's gradual unhingement.
I had collies to tend to
        and a victim of surgery,
legs splayed beside her crutches.
We talked and ate dog food in the kitchen
behind mood music
and the painful burning
        in such tortured love,
though it was not only that.

I could take a rhythm break
        in the wistfulness
of Brubeck and Desmond,
just listen
as if it were my pulse beating.
I won't do that.

The moon's bright and hard now,
full and dimensional,
        in the night's sky after rain.
There is no music in this reality after all,
just smoky scents from chimneys,
counterpoint to a dog's barking.

I think you might be happier,
less sleepy,
    if I told a story,
whether true or constructed
from degraded details:
hearts and flowers on a prom dress,
that kind of thing, Marie
    in 1953, before cappuccino,
sushi, and those other
        sophisticated trappings,
moon over the water and its river
upon the magic lake.
    It couldn't ever be casual,
a catalogue of names
followed us into our tents.
Then the deer came.
Or was it coyote, ferocious javelinas,
somebody's horse
    loose in the desert mountains,
a skunk caught in the trap we'd laid,
close to fatherless, Paul and I?

I saw him once later,
    married and gotten religion,
but then it was my dream, also a howling.
He crept into the tent
    quietly to soothe me,
himself too, since I was huffing
    and there might have been something
out there.
It was a dream of death wished for,
that I had brought ending
    to our absent fathers,
yet seemed more than a dream.

But Marie!
Hidden as the towhee sings tentatively
    and does not reveal herself
in the morning, light as the leaves
and brown tipped also
        in fall foliage,
what fragments of song can I call up
to soothe you, those degraded past tunes
of our ridiculous venture:
*Heart of my heart, I had the craziest dream,
Moon River?*

It seems even sinister
    now that the moon's glow
sings in the pines' candles, turning trees
to a semblance of women
        in spiky dresses or shrouds
set piecemeal
in the clear night beyond my window,
    just watching, or accusing me.
The song
might then be a dirge, though the tune
was once popular.

One more time: fish gotta swim,
birds fly,
    the bees get hooked
on pollen, myopically,
all the fragments seem in order,
like these pine trees
or that scent of eucalyptus,
        rancid still in virginity,
before it becomes cleansing
designer soap.

    I remember you
beyond justice or understanding,
as if we were reconstructed
to begin yet again,
a little bit of that longing,
        faint scent of romance,
the potion clarified now
in the music I thought then
       would focus and simplify
the shadow of your smile
and, in reality, the way I felt.

# Six Short Poems

## 1. Windsock

Sing windsock fall stars
      fret vacant eyes
in cloudy wing drifts
turning back to summer and you
new moon
level at horizon. Soon
      winter icing the shield
grease thickening our kind
shivering in cockpit's vacancy
of spring
which will never come
      to this sky's quarter
but will creep in
uncelebrated
      until we think ahead
to summer.


## 2. Passenger

Little unknown passenger once slung
diabetic candy on the shoulder
for balance
awhile to hold down chicory
      moving coffee mist
here in the mountains' freedom
from sickness
      of hanging bottles bandages
carabiner crutches a cane
that's sugar
parceled out in pyramids

     among trees under the sun
darkening the moon
glow in four hands joined
to form a stretcher
across the fire.


## 3. In Thrall

Tangible in regard to money's
     tuneful reversals new hat
worn down carefully
the style
of spending and getting
     brassy trombones rubber
planters a ring
for your delicate third finger
     last month's credit card bills
even the earth
held thrall to shopping
     a showplace
yet moving
beyond the static state
     of a breviary taken in hand
whose canonical hours
roll by over litter not rotting
but for caviar
forgotten in the fridge.


## 4. Dancing Shoes

Evermore in past hours
     on feet in dancer's shoes
buckled and high bows

    lyrical as that melody
played too fast
for this developing limp
   brought on by winter rain
soaking laces and various
metatarsus.
A story of worry fleshed out now
in time after times
   on the beach in the mountains
any court or dance
floor superior at such things
    though not others.
Animal magnetism the foxtrot lifting
its weary head
   to somebody else's feet
in the dancer's shoes
    goes by carefully noted
on the way of the world.


## 5. Fishing

Glandular regard
   of the stumblebums whose tents
along the river lift
in wind to settle once again
    after a good dinner
of crappie
and bluegill lunging at the bait cast
through great attention
free of reeds. Now soon after the wives
have gone down
   for civilized dancing
where the town's lights blink
in branches

of glorious promise
        urged on by camping
fishing manly eyes
on stars in the river
free now
and can talk like children.


## 6. Young Girl

It's late in the house and the girl
at summer's end in fire
      of fake hearth-logs purchased
from a boy stirring
something new yet remembered
in the tribe's life
of flesh repetitiously cooked up
            in centuries of the living
room where she now sits
      awkwardly cannot find
her spot.
Be still my foolish heart.

## Border Towns

Towns along the border
    seem to wake up when I enter them,
fresh squeezed
and hotcakes, or griddle
depending on which side you're on.
The thought of crossing over
        has me longing for return
almost immediately. Most often
there are fences, but not always
in mountains:
natural boundaries, fjords and gorges,
and sometimes there are troops
    at the demarcation
in defense or aggression,
gunboats even in narrow rivers.

I have not taken sufficient time
to mourn them,
    sent on their journeys
without backpacks or other accoutrements,
though I did creep up in the night
for a good look
before deciding on retreat.
    Borders are not benign mappings,
towns often seething like countries
before war.
I wished only to enter and then be gone,
but they had left things behind,
and I was stuck with them.

There,
at the gate marking the entrance
or the exclusion, there,

       given the sight lines,
crossing seems less than treacherous,
but coming back?:
that town
on the hill in the far distance,
       its warren of confusing streets.
I thought I had the answers
to all things measured, before departing.

Summer comes, then fall, then winter
       snow drifts against the barricades, [and] here
the ones who cover their ears up in the slightest breeze.
Should spring ever come again to this border town
[given the sight lines]
and those living without guile sufficient for dishonesty.
       To the one whose undergarments are soiled by sweat
and clots of blood in childbirth anciently
[before deciding], and to the derelict in the dead of winter,
her filthy hair, the ones [on retreat]
without energy for young children, their filthy hair.
       Should spring ever come forth again [in mountains]
to these tree skeletons and the girls who wish to dance,
       the square dance, the tango, the ones who dress
for winter even in the early fall.
[Depending on which side you're on], depending on the tune
of fire trucks and the strapping on of explosives, then
to the memory of burning leaves and the houses
ablaze in the burning, tree skeletons [without] and children
playing in the leaves [before war].
       [Not] unto the cold hammer, to the flesh under the hammer
[to mourn them], should spring ever come,
       but to the last effort, the final ditch, and the one
who stands romantic at the bedside in memory of seamen
and the pines spilling their hazy pollen [always]
in menses beyond the window and the soiled underwear.

[I have not taken sufficient time]
for the [borders are not] towns and the ones [sent on their
    journeys] stand guard at the gates, [its towns]
[in defense or aggression], nor for the dark soil
under the snow, the stink of compost, weather palaver,
and overheated radiators.
    The people stand in the town square, cold down even
to their private parts. [Most often] the officials
positioned [on the hill in the far distance]
    come to believe [almost immediately]
that the [crossing seems less than treacherous]. The fathers
who have no taste for the winter mothers and drink hot milk
with nutmeg as if they were children, bang each other
    on the shoulders and don't shave [for a good look].
And the fires are now burning
    in the [warren of confusing streets],
in the red hair of the ones under abuse and the sleeves
of the women dancing, on tables, in bones and long dresses,
who are the calaveras
who dance away death [at the gate marking the entrance
or the exclusion].
Never will spring come to [them], [hotcakes or griddle],
to the [towns]
    shivering in [benign mappings] of band formations,
ridiculous costumes and [other accoutrements], icy tuba
bells, [stuck with] epaulets, after marching to melodies
of mounted police music [before departing].
Fires [seem to wake up], as if in celebration of spring coming
[along the border], electric where [there are fences].
    Fires burn in the deep [gorges], on rafts upon [fjords],
as if the sun [had left] light behind [fresh squeezed]
in the night sky, left to [creep up in the night]
insanely, as converse [to all things measured] carefully
    [I thought I had the answers]
before attendant forgetting, to [that] talk as tumultuous

background, the noise [but] even of fruit flies
constant under that babble, orange stands [and] brass bands
[there] at the [town] center,
[but] ice under the hill, in the cracked cup,
in arthritic fingers and radiators, in trumpet valves,
shoelaces, all [things behind] in forgotten shadow
[when I enter them].
    [I wished only to enter and then be gone].
[But they], the fires, are burning along the fences
      having found a delineation at the scorched skin,
[and sometimes there are] pyres [seething
like countries] rising up against borders [there]
as if a dry flint struck for sudden ignition.
    All the towers are burning, the bridges,
[gunboats even in the narrow rivers] have been set aflame.
The houses and [backpacks] are burning, the churches,
    even the coffee shop I entered, [and I was]
in arrogance, at first light.
The snow is melting in the heat of burning
    at the barricade fences, [often] promising:
Perhaps it's spring!
[Or] all the borders are opening,
    but it's too late.
Even though people are running [coming back] swiftly,
their bodies burning
    as they pass others, also torches,
approaching the [natural boundaries],
    [troops at the demarcation],
[the thought of] their town entered [crossing over]
[has me] returning with them [though I did]
upon leaving, from the other side.

## Reversal of Fortunes

Beyond the orchestrated placement of the child's hands,
    fingers laced among seemingly strewn flowers,
in one of a number of cities
        where multitudes are allowed still to blossom,
men out of uniform at the periphery
photograph the bearers,
    whose burden seems light as a feather
and might actually rise up,
as borne on the Prophet's robes.

It's Sunday; it might be any day
in the recording,
everything soon to be solved,
and above the newspaper,
    hard rain holds acid in the early light
streaking my windows and disordered thoughts;
puddles rise into rivers
        along the gravel walkways,
stones vibrant and variously
multitudinous
as the world's children, as if bathed in oil.

    [Who would treat my body
to such soothing pleasure,
        sisters, mother, my grandmother?
Better to have felt my limbs in their hands
at some earlier time.]

    The grandmother once played by his gramophone,
a reversal of fortune, in a photograph
of a life spent wholesomely in a quiet town.

Bearers, can you spare a dime, for travel,
for the reversal of fortune of a child whose body
is quiet-town-wholesome, for a spent life?

[In a tape recording played by my grandmother],
on a gramophone, sisterhood to a spent life.
Is a dime given for quiet travel, wholesomely?

[I have nowhere to go, my grandmother's quiet town?]
The river reverses the fortunes of fishermen.
The streets become littered with bodies and gramophones.

The repetitious recording of the river is vicious
travel reversal of fortunes for spent children
who play gramophones along parkways and quiet streets.

[A dead town, a town for mothers] to spend life's dime.
Those who are wholesome are heard only on gramophones
or on tape recorders, spared for quiet travel reversals.

[If they had just oiled my ruined body, if they had just
laced long fingers between my piggy toes.]

The casual machine of childhood, a dime spun quietly
for travel, vicious restrictions, a tape's reversal,
so that one listens to fortunes spilling from grandmothers.

Or from rivers of gramophones, wholesome fishermen who are
tape recorders, unfortunate children along ruined parkways.
Each reversal turns littered streets to a spent quiet-town.

A dead town, a town of reversals and restrictions,
of life spent on rivers littered with spent fishermen,
broken recorders. [I have nowhere to play, for fortune.]

The body is lifted now casually into the sun;
    the grandmothers beat at their clothing.
Perhaps the flowers are falling
into the hair of the sisters,
    the mothers who stumble
into the cameras' perspectives.
But the bearers have been recorded,
these spent fishermen in this quiet town
    [a dead town] of reversals and restrictions.
I am fortunate in this stormy day,
these river pathways.

[If only it would rain
    to silence my grandmother and her gramophone,
to wash away this spent litter.
    If only they could spin
a dime for travel.]

My grandmother tells a story of reversal in a dead town,
a tape recording of the police chief, now a mortician,
his spent marriage, his son, his wife's gramophone.

[I fly for refuge unto the Lord of the daybreak],
to the dead-town marriage motel's violent restrictions
beside rivers littered with fortunes of dead children.

Reversal of a casual machine, the gramophone, multitudes
of pills to commemorate their union. [That He may deliver me
from the mischief of those things which He hath created.]

And rushes with his son on the spent dime, wholesomely
in the quiet town, passing rivers littered with fishermen,
tape recordings, photographs, everything soon to be solved.

No pills, but a barrel at her temple as the door opens again
and again, vicious repetition. [And let not compassion
toward them prevent you from executing the judgment.]

Now the litter is lowered down into the quiet town,
    the body wrapped up in the flowers,
child-size in the winding sheets.
        Yet the vicious recording continues
in photographs, gramophones of the grandmothers,
    tape recordings of the sisters.
A dead town of the mothers,
everything soon to be solved
        not by fishermen, seemingly strew flowers
on the unfortunate banks of reversed rivers,
not by the spinning of dimes spared
for quiet travel arrival
    into His taped presence
[who hath created man of congealed blood]
repetitiously recorded
in a litter of gramophones along spent parkways.

    A quiet town of police chiefs and morticians,
rivers along gravel walkways, vibrant and variously
multitudinous as the world's children bathed in oil.

    A dead town, a town of reversals and restrictions,
of violent fortunes in gramophones and honeymoon litter,
so that a wife can spin dimes for a smoking barrel.

The repetitious recording of the reversed river is vicious
highway of the bearers lifting burdens on the Prophet's robes.
Those who are wholesome are heard only on gramophones.

The casual machine of childhood travel, flying for refuge,
passing by parkways and rivers littered with spent fortunes.
The strewn fishermen, who might be fathers, are restricted.

Out of uniform at the periphery, photographs, on a dime spent
for litter of dead children, broken gramophones and mothers.
Sudden reversal of the casual machine, doth not prevent them.

[He will assist you against your enemies
      and will set your feet fast, but not for travel,
that reversal of a fortune in my piggy toes.
If they had just
      laced long fingers between them,
had oiled my body,
even with slick sludge
      in rivers littered from passage of His
amphibians through them,
who is provided with everything
and suffers not the work of any worker.]

The rain releases its fortunes into the dead town.
Petals fall like bright dimes into the sisters' hair.
The river reverses again and is cleansed of litter.

His grandmother's gramophone and tape recorder are spun
on a dime quietly, for travel, for maps of the town
no longer viciously restricted to men out of uniform.

No longer restricted to police chiefs and morticians,
their sons, and their wives reversing fortunes of pills
for smoking barrels at the doorways of marriage motels.

The casual machine of childhood, wholesome fishermen
beyond the barricades, everything soon to be solved.
The rain reverses the fortunes of the dead town's creation.

      A quiet town, rain water, burdens light as a feather.
In your last dream, He will lift you on the Prophet's robes
and will admit you into gardens, through which rivers flow.

## That's a Thought

Maybe I should drop you off,
park the car and walk back.
      Last time, I lost out.
If you will just
stay put, I can manage,
knowing which way to head.

I should drop you out, stay put,
and just manage last time.
      Knowing which way to head off,
I lost the car.
Maybe, if you will park, I can
walk back.

Park the car. I should stay put,
knowing I lost which way to head
      last time, walk back out,
just drop you off.
And maybe, if I can manage,
you will.

If you will just stay put,
knowing which way to head.
[too soon we are coming to grief]
      That's a thought
I can manage last time.
Maybe I should walk back,
[in a dark hysterical day]
drop you off and park the car.

Last time, knowing I should park,
[counting the hours waiting]
maybe drop you,

      if you will just stay put.
That's a thought.
[even when it was blood raining]
I could look around, walk back,
and manage which way to head.

[perhaps the city will soon be burning]
Surely, you'll be waiting.
Maybe I should drop you off and stay put.
      I could look around.
[all the leaders are without ethics]
That's a thought.
If you will just manage,
knowing which way to head back.

If you will stay put and manage, knowing
which way to head, I could look around.
      That's a thought,
[shamed by a crude arrogance]
stunned into somnolence.
Surely, you'll be waiting.
[assassination a commonplace]
Maybe I should drop back.

I could look around and maybe manage,
stunned into somnolence.
      Who's directing this traffic?
[hath not a penchant for understanding]
That's a thought I should drop, stay put.
Surely, you'll be waiting,
[the hammer of the iron will]
knowing which way to head.

Who's directing this traffic?
[birth unto ignorance unto death]

knowing which way to head,
    the outward sign,
stunned into somnolence: that's a thought.
[little time left for a quickening]
I could look around, maybe stay put
and manage. Surely, you'll be waiting.

Palaver of the cruel occupations, stunned
[the blind leading the blind]
into somnolence, the outward sign.
    Who's directing this traffic?
That's a thought. I could look around,
[unto this certain evil]
Surely, you'll be waiting, knowing
which way to head.

That's a thought, I could look around.
Surely, you'll be waiting,
    stunned into somnolence.
Who's directing this traffic?
The outward sign. Palaver of the cruel
occupations. Perhaps the city is burning.

Palaver stunned into the outward sign,
the cruel city is burning,
    I could look around this,
the thought surely of directing a somnolence.
Who's waiting? Perhaps you'll be.
Occupations, that's traffic.

Perhaps you'll be around. I could look.
The outward traffic is burning.
    That's a thought waiting somnolence
of the city sign,

surely stunned into the occupations.
Who's directing this cruel palaver?

Too soon we are coming to grief
in a dark hysterical day,
            counting the hours waiting
even when it was blood raining.
        Perhaps the city will soon be burning.
All the leaders are without ethics,
shamed by a crude arrogance.

Assassination a commonplace,
hath not a penchant for understanding
            the hammer of the iron will.
Birth unto ignorance unto death,
        little time left for a quickening,
the blind leading the blind
unto this certain evil.

## Gallery

A child standing before a blackboard.
    A ragamuffin standing before a stone wall.
Something is given: a hand, a mask, a piece of chalk.
There, in the left side of the chest.

Having deciding on a honeymoon trip fashioned
    for other parties, flowers in her hair.
Figures only from maps upon arrival.
To the right side facing a child, underhanded.

Something is cast aside: a ring, a knife, a garter.
    Ghost of dalmatian's head above the cowcatcher.
Having expected another vehicle entirely.
Fire in awakening on the station platform.

Only to find it is time now for sleeping.
    A child high in the air over water.
As much as they have carved out and anticipated.
Having discovered little in this pipe dream.

Something discovered in the dark zone.
    Under the sternum: a tin can, strapping, a bomb.
A child's arm high in the air over water.
Electricity's burst at the architect's window.

Limping down a country path at the dead end of summer.
Frail asters, a ragamuffin, pathetic rear guard.
    The bride stands flushed at the gate.
Something on the ground: a ring, a skeleton traveler.

A party fashioned only for strangers.
    The groom stands at the gate in a fur hat.

Ice-crusted pines through a foggy window.
The other: gone south into sinister places.

Against onslaught of that winter's coming
    in a frosty train down from a distance.
Pipes and hot tea, something burning.
A child dancing in electrified tethers.

Of a country garden: cans, bolts and wires.
    Something among the living at the bride's feet.
Tea, in degrees dipping through the narrow windshield.
[Did I mistake this for a real romance?]

In the aftermath of the war the war continues.
    A child selling the news before a barricade.
[someone like you]
After the fallen bride: on the ground, a ring.

Festival Dancers dead in their tracks at the ceremony.
    The architect moves in sludge to the window's map.
There, in the left side of the chest.
[I wish I knew]: something on the ground, frail asters.

The wish set forth on a train into the future.
    Figures only from maps upon arrival.
[if you don't care]
Skeletons dance in the Festival Dancers' outfits.

Having expected another vehicle entirely.
[But you can only answer me]: a thing, a piece of metal.
    This, picture of the ground on which . . .
Fire of the groom dancing in flames at the ceremony.

After the declarations [I wish I knew], marriage or war.
    The child stands before walls, vehicles, borders.

He carries the bride into the honeymoon chamber.
Having discovered little in this pipe dream.

Returning then into shelter after the blood-rain.
    The groom slakes passion in drink from a decanter.
Something discovered in the dark zone.
[What should I do?]: this ground, asters, oil.

[Don't lead me on if I'm a fool to say so.]
    The bride stands flushed at the gate.
On the ground. Always on the ground. Under the ground.
The river bears up the dead, still in their costumes.

A party fashioned only for strangers.
    A child standing at judgment before a stone wall.
[Should I keep dreaming on or just forget you?]
At the southern end of the city, flames.

The bride washing herself seen through a foggy window.
    A child dancing in electrified tethers.
The coach comes down, bearing the skeleton figures.
On the ground, something: [I wish I knew.]

The station, ruined in fire in the architect's window.
    Something among the living at the bride's feet.
[Why let me hope and pray so?]: a ragamuffin, a child.
It stands, falling over in the river, its arm in the air.

[You'd place no one could love one above me.]
    In the aftermath of the war the war continues.
The bride is pictured standing against a blackboard.
A ruined map, the ground sucking up all evidence.

The earth is soddened as the mind is with memory.
    The train bears the calaveras in the dancers' costumes.

Having placed the child pressing against a post.
All the barriers. The ground breaking. [I wish I knew.]

In the dark cistern, in the powder puff, delight or death.
    To have ironed out all problems and costumes.
Of the river. In the river. Fallen over.
After we were about to begin again in travel.

The bride and groom. Festival Dancers. The architect.
    Having planned a trip into the south knowing no risk.
Asters strewn on the ground before the garden gate.
Something: a wet hankie, a flag rising as a child's arm.

In time after time is spent the coin and the oil.
    A ragamuffin hangs only as a doll for the news.
The bride is pictured standing beside the groom.
The skeletons dance away flesh at the festival.

## Dolls

Little maiden cares so little
for love that when
    her doll breaks open
it's for lost power of manipulation
that she weeps
as much as nursing game.

What innocence has she learned
to set aside
in this cruel world
    for maidens and an evil one
of doll-maker fabricators
who are politicians
forcing through budgets
for weapons?

And war doth not temper them. I saw
the doll face of a child
where she had fallen,
    not as beautiful as the living,
piggy toes pointing
at the smoky sky.

Just as they have come to regard each other
wearily, these lessons are handed down
even to maidens.

And these other dark dolls,
whose toys are cans,
    electrical wires, bolts,
might they let them alone in their playing,
or will they too break open?

## Prayer to the Most Powerful Hand

I place my Christian soul before thee
fundamentally, to rid myself of it,
    this despair and anguish,
light the candle
beseechingly against
ruined feet, rescue, devotion,
this destiny of suffering
    that is not mine or theirs,
those "sacred" and profane hearts.

A hand up and a handling
of wonders, loving kindness. But your hand
    becomes a fist, then a hammer,
a sledge in the shape of a book, your
palm on the cover, stigmata,
drives down the homeless, even more
those who are hungry,
for what: faith, belief, surcease
of sorrow? But for food, shelter, shoes,
electricity, water, not
for loving kindness. Justice of Democracy?
What is that here,
    but to be pounded more firmly
under power of hysterical arrogance.

Hand,
come down upon the self-righteous,
    down as a hammer in retribution
upon the "sorrowful hearts"
in their impossible ignorance
and the acid of their ministrations.
    But you will not come down.
Let us pray upon forgiveness,

for strength and wisdom,
for pardon from a destiny of suffering
brought by these limp and fattened wizards
in hiding behind your palm.

    Let us pray in the name of
the most powerful hand
and the fundamental testament.
Then let us close the book that is a hammer
and walk out of the churches forever,
though we be initially blinded
in eternal sunlight and drink sparingly
from the clear pool of forgetfulness
as you wave us away.

    — from the inscription on a holy candle

# A Cole Porter Medley

## 1. I Concentrate on You

Gray skies and winter winds,
so people declare surrender once again
        [an ev'ry time, we say]
on the tender decline,
and blues become the so-so concentrate
too strong to brew: [of] you
and men, [but] on the intertwine.
        Our trouble begins in your eyes dream,
[goodbye] never to prove sweet fortune wise.
Whenever true,
whenever to me wrong, [there's time,
we know] comes through you even on [a] song.
        [Be] your smile, first kiss to me;
you're my only concentrate.
Look, my arms. I can be wise to you
when men say, nay –
        that love's young.
I become light when at that concentrate,
whenever I concentrate
on you.

## 2. Don't Fence Me In

Oh send me to the ridge
        where cottonwood trees ride [on] the moon.
Let me gaze at the wide land, murmur, and wander
off to forever underneath the mountains.
        I can't [concentrate and] fence the stand
of open country,
[nay] western skies above.
Can't [I] rise to straddle the fences in me?

[When you] listen, look at [me]
    the hobbles. Let me in.
Don't give me
    the evening breeze on lots of starry skies.
I want my cayuse, my old saddle, over yonder,
under the land that I don't love.
    Let me be myself, lose my senses [and you].
Don't fence till I see
    [when] the West commences.
Please, don't ride thru me.
Just turn me loose.

## 3. Ev'ry Time We Say Goodbye

Strange, the gods, little lark
    somewhere in the air above me,
you're near [me] to [let me]
begin [in] spring
    ev'ry time I die
from the change to minor.
[I ask you] must we say goodbye?
[But] I wonder a little why
    I allow you to [fence me in], go
sing finer,
[till I] say major about it
[in] no love song.
How they think of me when, so little,
there's such a goodbye [fence]
about it.
    Who can hear ev'ry why?
Ev'ry single time
we say goodbye.

NOTE: Every word of each refrain (and only these) is used in the poems. Residual words from 1 enter 2 in brackets, and so on in a circle.

## Too Late Now

Carefully, but any time [too late]
    the flesh in carelessness
[now to forget]
places itself, distracting [your smile]
       upon the hearth
or in memory [the way] of pain
[one word] calls out,
the hour then rolls around [makes]
    in which the marker [my heart]
of lost capability can shine
and [rejoice] then, only to close
      [close] down [darling, no]
fragments [danced awhile],
    I am urged on to the clock,
though [imagine myself]
       release temporary suffering
under this burden of chopped ice
[anymore].

Forgetfulness, [the way we cling]
after the bad [done] deed,
    after [tender] discovery,
what is this but loss and perversity
of freedom, my hand not on the
      hearth then, but stung
in abuse of another [stays]?
To return [and be the same
    as I was before] and go before judges,
but [someone new] yet to remember
the body, the sting, slamming
[the door].

Yet for reward, passionate as the clock,
tumblers dropping in the lock,
    [to forget and go on] for this
[I relive] in remembrance of [your voice]
your shocked face, I
turn not [away from you]
to the crimes. Whatever the hammer,
    the red hearth [my heart], that soothing
of chopped ice in sink
or bucket, [all the things] it's no good
to count days and hours,
    to measure against
some chart of the possible
[when we're apart]
and not very likely [together].
It lives [on in] only in the textures,
[too late now] to confuse [fun]
with some distant idea
    of seriousness, [to forget]
which is life's illusion [too late]
arrived at [now] in anger,
    [now] in laughter, [to] go
and then [to] return, refreshed
saying [how could I ever] I'm sorry [now],
though it was [too late]
and well after.

Sustenance,
[when we've] returned for cruelty,
    [all the] hard times awaiting us
[together] yet amount to nothing
in light of this.
Mark it down on the chart, let the
tumblers fall.

After coming a good long way,
[we've] let the mix of ice and hearth
continue. The clock strikes [no]
    the hours and days,
imagines a time when it will all
be over. [I can't] It's too late now
[It's too late now].

## My Little Plane

1

Perhaps the air will let
my little plane down
to sink into that imprint
on the land in the lens's watermark
finally upon paper
      which is a map impossible
of that size for understanding like
me and my mom like it was awesome
in a language inadequate
      unto the darklight
and the warning light at the door
developing what can never be approached
in the shadow
under the shadow.


2

I saw a woman hidden in a lava
declivity
      my little plane's shadow
at the periphery near a bowl
of water stagnant in blue absence
      of past activity or perhaps
it was a man impossible to be certain
in a language inadequate
from this altitude
      was missing or lost love
that unspecified yearning
developing what can never be approached
as I was working my way
back to you.

3.

Adventure of the shadow of my little plane
fixed on film and in the memory
    of a hovering over sea
though it was land looking like waves
from this altitude
and higher still were daystars
also invisible in
        that unspecified yearning
for a past deeper in some other anatomy
that I might be touching
though only through shadows
of myself behind uncertain lenses
    in this constant droning
of the engine like the world's turnings.


4.

So then was traveling through smoke
above such archeology
      which is a plundering
like me and my mom
    like it was awesome figures
from a past inadequate
in this constant droning
of a language
that I might be touching
you on the earth bound up
in complexity ancient as memory
    of a time fashioned from childhood
when we stepped fresh from the cockpit
at least it seemed that way.

5.

Ice threatens before fire
    under the warming
of my little plane's shadow
and hearth light aglow there beckoning
you on the earth bound up
    in such glacial imagination
could freeze into a fixture
to then percolate
in this heated nostalgia
at least it seemed that way
high up as I was
thinking to fall
    down into animal memory
inhuman and finally alone.


6.

Two thousand over big island skylight
thinking to fall
    as much wish as a dream
of my little plane casket descending
into the orange eye
    to then percolate
in the blue field
which is night's hoard and endless
like it was awesome like
    a gestural language without
me and my mom like turning
into a past absent
of all memory sufficient
unto nostalgia.

7.

Like it was awesome like
a valley smoking its own anatomy
         under which another surface
of a kind of skin
peeled back and revealing
            yet another no longer
a mystery but a shadow
under a shadow
of all memory sufficient
         unto the task forgotten
as I was drifting in the realization
that the lens too is a false framing
the world's turnings myopic
in the watermark stain of my little plane.


8.

Like me and my mom like were walking
through a desert and came into
         a mystery but a shadow
to cool us as we looked up finding
the little plane casting a watermark
down upon us who were trying
            hard to give vent to our
broken relationship in this wilderness
unto the task forgotten
         as I imagined myself in the plane
my shadow a stain to provide like an awning
to give her some comfort
correct for a son or a daughter yet I
in another story entirely.

9.

We were looking out to a far horizon
like me and my mom were like inside
    in another story entirely
a Rothko painting of the earth's hues
in changing greens and the sky's blues
over Brittany coming
        down upon us who were trying
to right our relationship in the cockpit
of my little plane
which of itself was fragility drifting
    almost invisible in a soup
like Rothko's paint like me and my mom
the whole sky was an awesome home
and we were at comfort in it.


10.

Under the shadow of lava in the lens
perhaps a father awaits me as a lover
almost invisible in a soup
    crowded with images existent only
in this sentimental and foolish eye
but to each his own
        and the earth is beautiful if violent
and can be like me and my mom
like I can be a baby girl or boy again
and wouldn't that be awesome
    but like very painful
and I brought my eye back to the cockpit
only to find I was there and here
which of itself was fragility drifting.

11.

Imagine the water a shadow figure
in this sentimental and foolish eye
      the land a face seen from a satellite
youth the green beyond the ancient cuts
like plastic surgery
      to bring youth back
and wouldn't that be awesome
though having suffered for the gain
supposing violence
      of time could be forestalled
before the figure under the shadow
becomes finally fixed
and the sea no more than a blue wash
spied in the lens.


12.

The human past is dead
      though this earth rise up violent
and beautiful red in the lens
to bring youth back
      like me and my mom
before the figure under the shadow
is revealed
      as a surface of blue only
to be peeled back revealing another
surface on which we can't be stable
      though continue the drift
in the lens of imagination
and if it be still of the human past
let it.

13.

On the way always as a returning
      as a surface of blue only
in the distance becomes water
beyond parching
          as life giving
sustenance of the destination
is revealed
though only for this brief pausing
      and not for satiation
which is temporary
respite in the journey
          like me and my mom
like awesomely back there
at the beginning.


14.

Finally upon paper
of past activity or perhaps
      fixed on film and in the memory
above such archeology
          in this heated nostalgia
which is night's hoard and endless
under which another surface
the little plane casting a watermark
      like me and my mom were like inside
but like very painful
though having suffered for the gain
to be peeled back revealing another
as life giving
on the way always as a returning.

## Roughly There

Turning back to mark the spot
where she was standing,
          branches having formed
in my absence a canopy
     or ceiling, filtering noon light
to become a kind of evening,
causing me to stumble
at the crest where she went over
and almost
back in her company again,
     I was able to pause, hold on,
and take stock of things.

She was standing there, roughly
where you are now.
     The tragedy, I thought,
that all her fruits should be of labor
and only I left to record them
and her termination.
          Just stepped over . . .
Out in the air only for moments . . .
     A fall, before sudden stop . . .
The story is driven
          in search of a reason.
For the public, chalk it up
to accident.

Where you are now,
a purse tossed in the grass,
     glasses, a scarf blown back
to flutter
on that branch before I retrieved it:
          tangible leavings

to make something of.
The purse was a cloth handbag,
    glasses on the National Health,
the scarf, Armani.
        What did you say, a storm?
On the cliffs here
there are many, but not that day.

The Princess at work in the keep
counting out coins,
    hammering at the kiosk,
no more leverage.
We had gone dancing the night before
and the child was still stuttering.
    You didn't know of the child, the heir?
His is buried where you are,
roughly there.

[I did know. Hands fingering my hair,
the tale told.]

Dramatic deaths in the telling, the docent,
when the boy came in with the multitudes,
    to learn of his parents,
both fallen from grace in adultery,
the castle haunted
    and now invaded,
tourists touching the dusty fabrics,
looking in to forbidden rooms.

    We lived in the far wing, somewhat
isolated. She kept
the keep and the boy safe, her sister his mother
and the real Princess, riches
    to be handed down at his maturity,

and in the meantime, tourists,
    the admissions kiosk
being built then at the barbican,
this castle the size of a small city.

[And in that city, our assignations,
bodies draped over dust covers
upon opulent furniture
        below tapestries. My scarf
in use erotically, then given up to her,
Armani, now memento mori.]

Pleased to remember the final night
we danced together,
    no care for coin after the first
flush of invasion. They came in droves,
anxious for tangibles,
        that brush and comb,
table and place setting of the final meal,
his suit worn on that fateful day,
replicas of the knife
and poker the police took away.
    The boy beamed and lost his stutter
temporarily.
I saw him, from where I was often hiding,
behind heavy drapes
and velvet ropes in the drawing room.
    The docent winked at him,
who was coming
to some enlightenment.

[We too went dancing,
    in the unreconstructed ballroom,
ruins of a bandstand,
fractured tables on low risers, ripped away

velvet, and the smell of rancid wax.
    A tape recorder played our tunes softly,
songs of better times,
there in our quarter in the castle city,
cousin. I was the docent, in disguise.]


    She became his mother after the tragedy
of the dead sister I had courted
before our marriage
    and the moving in with them,
she, the boy, and her husband,
all of them drawing me, each in their way
to wickedness,
    and perhaps my Princess
saw this early on,
in dancing . . . glancing . . .
    in the way I'd lost
out to a gold digger pharmacist,
    in my attentions to the lad,
though I'd refused her children
from the very start.
You'll understand all this,
your credentials as a biographer.


[As a docent, I was bringing him
to an understanding,
    fates of the castle made public
in her extremity.
The coins were listed in denominations,
each one squeezed.
    Then there was this other accounting.
In the meantime
rolling around with each other
    in relief of financial anxiety,
and I came to love her.]

Not for love or money
have I come here again with you.
    The scarf reminds me
something else was afoot.
It was Armani
and now locked safe in the keep
as memento mori.
A possibility of some vague retribution?
    She and the boy are dead.
I'm wealthy.
You can write that down, but the other
shall remain, always, a mystery:
    the knife and poker,
the brush and comb,
his pockets
stained by the pharmaceutical chemicals he always carried
and spoke about incessantly. One of them
    suddenly hungry for a meal other than that provided,
though it was pheasant that night,
white truffles
    the boy wouldn't eat, his stomach
and throat twisted
in awareness that something
was quite definitely not right.

    Her hands then
pressed the table in her rising,
having excused herself. She'd passed
the poker in her leaving,
    then came back to stand behind him
before she went.
Maybe he saw my eyes above his head.
    He was gripping the carving knife
and turning.
The boy was watching, his stutter
just beginning.

[My hair in the brush and comb,
    a set of tortoise her sister
had handed down. Is that in the keep too,
wrapped up carefully in the scarf?
The boy saw only the violence.
    As a docent, it was up to me
to provide the history
and cure the stutter. I was curing her
also at that time.
    We came to arrange ourselves
on pews below stained glass renderings
    in the chapel: virgins
and winged children.]

So it's a stand off, I mean
    here we are where she stepped over.
He might have been cuffed across the temple
with the replica poker
    I imagine in mid-stutter
and sudden grief at her leaving. Then,
almost magically, I became the last heir.
    He's roughly there,
almost below your feet.
    It could have been
the branch were the scarf was hanging
and not the poker,
    as he was reaching
out to save her.
You can write that down.

[And write down, too, the end of lives
    in a castle large as a city,
write something about her body,
not for publication,
    the love of a distant cousin.

All retribution
comes 'round again in a bloody circle
within these castle walls,
the barbican a tower to keep it in.
    "The last one shall be first,"
appropriately,
since we were rolling around
            in a chapel to give her succor,
impossible I learned,
when she had informed me of her plans,
then handed down the potion
        the pharmacist left behind:
to step over . . .
out in the air only for moments . . . ]

        She and the boy are dead.
I'm wealthy.
Let us return now for a quiet dinner,
pheasant and white truffles,
in the reconstructed banquet hall.
    The tourists are gone,
the barbican's a guard tower once again.
I've given the servants the night off.
We'll eat by candlelight.
            You can ask questions.
Maybe then
we can do some other things together.

[Only time will tell.]

## Two Drunks

So sorry
to have nudged the lapidary cases;
you were a stunner, and after swimming
in bourbon after swimming
     you were momentarily your ankles,
ass over teakettle at the bed side.
Nothing to be gained, actually,
but balance,
for I might have fallen down too
and crushed you in hysterical laughter.
         How romantically lustful
we might have been
that day, even remembered
being decorated:
onyx, opal, diamond, emerald.
It might have taken my breath away.

# Lockout

Careful, in my turning of the key
    [separated by a door]
though I was satisfied
to be locked out [after long absence]
there was something in oil
[and old glycerine]
to promise, yet prevent entrance.
    [All that time traveling]
to you beyond thoughts of you
[exotic places]
since I had spent countless hours
    [in towers, fortresses,
foreign tongues] without elsewhere,
thinking of a room behind me
[redecorated] closed
against my arrival as I was before
    [a single bed now, colorful
new fabrics]
banished, even in the locks of this town.
[What, exactly, did you expect?]
Homecoming,
    [the laying down of your head
upon the same pillow] studious
excuses [a welcome mat?],
brotherhood, though you are no sister,
    [if I should remember]
times in the cafe [old songs]
*the shadow of your smile*
    [responsible]
those adolescent correctives
[heart felt].
The hours, the days, the messengers,
the perfumed letters [mine]

      and the pleasures of learning
[now this]
that I have brought back to reward you
      [for waiting] in a head
longing for that pillow,
      tilted, here at the door. [Take it
and the rest away now.
I have been as bored as wood].

## Cairo

Upon conclusion of the light fantastic
    and before the steamer trunk
wound up in Cairo,
there were at least a half dozen women
to consider in imagination
or memory in the small cabin.

Let's see: mother,
Old Aunt Edith, the two evil sisters
    and the younger, sweet one,
then the *Chinoise* triplets, two-thirds,
who had followed
when the bar closed down at twelve;
    they spoke "impeccable" English,
yet liked to be addressed in tandem
this way: C-2 and C-3. That's seven
and not six,
and there was one other.

What transpired:
first, some were sober,
    sweet little sister, mother
and the triplet I might have danced the tango with
for a good part of the evening.
Old Aunt Edith
    lurched about
in surface dreams in her rocker,
influence of brandy?,
and the sisters, in their evil ways,
    were trying to tell one from the other.
Sure, we'd danced the night away,
often cheek to cheek,

        but it was hard to figure identity
in another place.

The evil ones had been dancing too,
always together,
        and I'd had a few turns with little sister.
The three others were wallflowers.
        The band, a little awkward in sea swell,
was called The Cairo Express,
though the boat was heading down the porch steps,
a toy upon imagined rapids,
*en route* to some benign island near the street.
                And the wallflowers? My mother,
Old Aunt Edith, one of the *Chinoises*.
Is it confusing? I was. What about the other?

Second: "It bubbled up along the curbing,
a simmer; how can this be water? Night Life
        in party hats and condoms,
a toy boat riding a dead rat
and moving
        slowly for the sewers
under street musicians
packing up their saxophones and tubas.
        It was August, no French along the *Seine*,
inside the *Louvre*, the *Beaubourg*,"
all those stupefying place names. Was it
one of the *Chinoises*
who'd said she'd not been there for a while,
or was it a whisper
from the trunk itself,
        a scraping as the porter dragged it
down the hard wood steps,
along the sidewalk and the grass verge
heading for the gutter?

The messenger of mortality forgets the story,
the details, *that* one,
stepping forth from desert dunes
      or down a steep metal stairway, shrouded
in steam at the old train station,
who is ragged
      from journeying, his own story,
and reconstructs the other,
          little doilies cut from cloth
and the antimacassar from Aunt Edith's rocker.
He'd hand them ahead
to the one who has decisions
about public consumption,
      but the chest holding the evidence,
upon camel or in baggage car,
has gone somewhere,
      hijacked or uncoupled,
sent to another destination, a mistake
in itinerary.
It might as well be Cairo.

Close in the cabin and crowded,
the trunk at the bulkhead,
somebody's smoking hemp at the porthole.
      "It's our turn now!":
the evil sisters
in their behaviors, in bad postures,
      hands fumbling in the fabrics of their dresses.
The boat bobs down from the final step,
then steams along the grass verge
approaching the gutter.
A faint knocking at the hatch.

      Old Aunt Edith
lurches awake from dreaming,

"Is that the porter?"
One of the *Chinoises* is yearning
    for the missing C.
Sweet little sister commences to weep.

All along I've been traveling
to a destination,
the trunk to precede me as treasure,
    not to Paris or Cairo, but that gutter.
And when I get there?: transgressive,
in danger,
    embraced at the storm drain
by mother, my little boat
gone down in the flow.

But third: the other,
the interloper, the missing sister,
a *Chinoise* cook,
    those slippery midnight eels
and crispy chicken feet in batter,
    dumplings steaming under silver hoods
on the gueridon. Cuttlefish?,
ancient eggs in aspic,
delectable dominos of uncertainty.
Little sister
    weeps for conventional porridge.
It's morning.
She wants toast, jam and milk.
The evil sisters will eat most anything.
Aunt Edith
    has fallen back into dreaming.
Mother is sleeping.
One of the Cs is ready,
    once again, for dancing, the other
fumbles in somebody's clothing.

In advance of arrival, the trunk is gone,
rich scent of hemp at the porthole.
The bow bumps at the dock's fenders.

Or was it cement at the cracked sidewalk?
The messenger is bleeding out memory.
    "They walked, misdirected
through the Cairo streets, baksheesh, and doors opening
surreptitiously into the dark mosques.
        Then they crossed back over
the highway, a dangerous crossing,
and returned, through the hatch,
to find the cabin empty."
        I might as well have been
the messenger of mortality
myself.

A dangerous crossing:
the steps, the grass verge,
      the sidewalk, the curb. The little boat
bobs in the journey. The gutter
        approaches, a simmer, can this
be water? I lean at the storm drain.
    The sisters are watching,
Old Aunt Edith.
The boat moves and the land doesn't.
Scooped up, then, by mother.

Light as a feather, the memory
    of the boat descending, light
as the future,
the chest holding memories of the past.
      How seldom the rising up of the image
of the lost boat in dream
or imagination of the hours of the child

spent in childhood: that vagueness
    of danger, loss, love, impossible
journeys on steps and concrete,
heading for arrival at rivers, *Seine*,
        Nile, or the simple mid-west gutter
at flood tide after a spring rain.
My blond hair was long
    like a girl's hair
in the photograph, mother in love
with a girl,
herself to begin again,
    to do it over again,
because the chest was lost or empty.
How can I now begrudge her,
my grey hair falling at the crown?

Evening, landlocked,
and the day spent in snoozing.
    Old Aunt Edith and the evil sisters
up and around. Where's mother,
little sister, the two *Chinoises*?
Maybe
we've put the past behind us, dancing,
    fumbling around in clothing,
that odd banquet in the morning hours.
Mother has gone ashore for shopping.
    Little sister is in the casino
playing pachinko. The *Chinoises*
have walked out into the boulevards
to practice French.
The little boat's gone down the drain.

If I am sleeping, if
    I am safe, still, in my bed,
it is because of the journeying,

the messenger of mortality remembering,
though piecemeal.
I was scooped up by mother,
        that dangerous crossing,
who is now shopping only
to return again.

One last time: mother, Old Aunt Edith,
the two evil sisters
        and the little sweetie. Three *Chinoises*,
the dancer, one other, and the cook.
Don't forget the porter,
        though in the end it's no matter
that the trunk is lost forever,
somewhere in Cairo.

## Foolish Heart

The blush on memory recalled
still sumptuous
as clerical robes cast aside,
the Soldier of Jesus
        unto the handmaiden,
those buckles and bows so
artfully available,
then said his baby prayers.

Bless us and keep us,
       on his knees at bedside in pajamas,
chin on the coverlet;
         and keep too the lost lovers
in pilgrimage,
though hearts be reluctant to start.

Genevieve, that's a name
       fascination as a lovely tune
sung foolishly into the night's
sensation.
         Is that pose painful?
Could we manage the same
dream combinations
and not be embarrassed by our bodies?

The scene is set for dreaming, knocking
at little doors
as in the Advent calendar:
braces behind
        bruised lips
behind the first one,
then Genevieve, much younger.
A door each day,

  but there's a land
between that's hard to see.

So what, that we were innocent
most usually,
  that will fade and fall apart,
foolish lips eager magic
lost and no longer believed in.

On an evening such as this,
Genevieve, fire starter, ever constant,
  the moon was too close,
white light.
Beware.


2.

Love's at the heart fooled before
  fascination. It isn't
take care, that blush
still sumptuous. So what,
constant moon,
that we were given
  the scene innocent. Beware,
Genevieve, braces to cut lips
eagerly foolish
  hearts on an evening sensation
to spend time, white light
reluctant
of statuesque poses,
night like
  incarnation.
On knees at bedside in pajamas,
clerical robes
  cast from the maiden

beside available chin
        on the coverlet, eager
embarrassment, each day the door
dreamed a fire
of buckles and bows.


3.

Bright future intractable
     little lord given to loss
sung foolishly,
lips eager magic, the kiss
statuary.
Is that pose painful?
Bless us and keep fascination's
       scene set for reluctant pilgrimage.
So what, that we were innocent
chin on the coverlet,
       buckles of reluctant soldier
in pajamas
though hard to see.

On an evening such as this,
constant moon,
it's the Genevieve dream,
     handmaiden
artfully available
at little doors.

Beware white light,
     baby prayers, the blush
on memory constructed
still sumptuous.
       It's a name sensation.
That's time,
my foolish heart.

## Standard-17, Some Other Time

Buds popping in the garden
      fed by a recent rain, your hair
fed by "gutsy." All the plants are poking
up on a scale of grey to green.
            Is this the current fashion?
Let's make light of it: my hair
      conditioned by the air
is why I wear a cap
         to watch the lettuce closely,
for it will soon turn bitter
beyond maturity.

Not only
      when something comes to mind
but any time
clouds darken this horizon;
maybe we should move to Florida,
      get a condo and a chair
with soft cushions.
         Some other time.
There seems to be enough left for decisions
called up in the lens,
      though wanting only a little
in this presence now.

A border of flowers, cut carefully
at the edges, beyond which
      the unruly,
paint peeling
and the cracked caulking, so much
to be tending;
      guess I'll water these flowers,
pull a few weeds,

        just ramble along
until you've awakened:
"Good morning" and coffee
        in this blessed pavilion,
the new day
but a token of continuance.

Fire remembered in the eucalyptus,
the ambulance still shuddering at the smell.
        Somebody's moaning early,
a woman in her nightgown in the grass.
Or do I confuse
        the cut corpse of a baby girl,
her incision closed with safety pins,
when I was needfully
in violation, and the doctor too
was pale?

It's in the nature of things,
days seem to be racing,
        comes the time for parting
just when things were starting.

Back down the road at Fairyland
        somebody threw up in the bucket ride,
the cleaning left to the operator.
Let's bring on the sick and injured
in comparison to the dead
some other time.

Old rags in the basement
and a moldy shirt,
        some faded Hawaiian pattern, palms
and a pelican.
        Though I had never been there,

I must have been thin then.
    And that raggedy red towel,
where did that come from?

Haven't done half the things we want to
    and the other half forgotten.
We'll never catch up completely.
Oh, well . . .
    rambling with the roses,
yet to avoid these thorns,
        will decorate the pavilion
any rainy day.

Remembering Santa Fe,
a recent trip to warm our bones,
    though it was cold in the mornings.
Each event's eroding,
        those museums on the hill,
the taste of dinner, twice?,
at the Mucho Gusto.
    I remember you,
but not the words unspoken,
not even the talking,
    though that sand-set silver bracelet
is vivid and still here.
There was something,
quietly said, before we bought it.
Let's be glad
    for what we've had,
though soon forgotten,
just as a late reward turns up
from a gift given without attachments.

    This brooch, that other pin,
this feral music

accurate only in the accounting.
Where has the time all gone to?

The loop of a miniature railway tracking
its figure eight,
    a child's pleasure in repetition,
but she was a baby girl
closed up with safety pins.

A woman in her nightgown in the grass,
gutsy in the wind in pretense
to lift her flowered cape,
    but only a nightgown really;
who would be out so early,
under the fiery eucalyptus trees
in morning dew?
        A dramatic picture,
the feral music,
weeping for a short past,
    a seemingly endless future.
She's held together still
    with safety pins,
the flesh
now unfeeling, but nonetheless.

    Conflation of her brows
into a single line,
cause for alarm or the expression thereof,
    urgency of time left for embracing
only her clothing now, this fabric
cross-handed at her elbows.
        We can never catch up
in emblems
moving only in memory's erosions.
Too many words are still unspoken.

I'll bring roses
into the blessed pavilion.
    Life goes on, or it doesn't,
even on the brink of starting.
Oh, well,
    this day's just beginning
and whatever's
        to come forth from it,
even a ghost story
of a child reassembled,
    life still in these magic fingers
as if passing the oxygen.

Optimal in regard to music,
    whose tunes then would remind us,
a captain or a princess,
a king roaming this property?
        Only a passenger for a while
on the figure eight loop,
though various spurs and dead-ends:
a failed marriage,
    embarrassments and bad company.
I'm thankful for erosion.

What was it we did exactly
in Puerto Rico?
I remember the battlements,
    protection from sea assault
anciently, the coffee,
something about your posture
on a balcony,
not quite captured in the photograph.

It's not the memory that links us,
    even those songs are held isolate,

lyrics to be taken quite seriously
at some time or another.
There's a moon over Miami,
        but I refuse to go there.
Old devil moon, too, in windows
in this blessed pavilion
and so much more
        in the manner of music,
hoofing the light fantastic
to Moonglow, Miller's Mood Indigo,
craziest dream,
        even on these heavy feet.

Dampened by morning dew,
        fire eating the oxygen,
her gown's held at the shoulders
with safety pins
        and the baby disassembled
right here:

absent of breath, her skin's perfect
as the Blue Moon, lying there
as we all shall do, no longer sleeping.
        White powder on my gloves, green
at the gills, hesitant
        before reaching out to close her up
with safety pins.

It was simply to make mention
        of the dead and the dead without names,
though she of course had one,
        no time to grow into it
but in thoughts
raggedy as that dew dampened nightgown.

I seem to remember it rained then,
    "to mingle with her cold tears,"
but this was California,
in summer, and that's hardly possible.

    Perhaps it was Arizona
when they set fire
to a dead horse in the mountains,
    that feral scent
of scorched leather, gone up in smoke
like memory,
though I'm sure of the cold morgue
and the safety pins.

I wanted only
    a little rambling, some watering,
a few yanked out weeds;
just passing the time until you awakened
and the blessed pavilion
found its order, on track again in the sun.
    Oh, well, some other time.
There seems to be enough left
to start forgetting.

# Feather

Tripping the light fantastic
when the air is so soft.
    Do bugs turn over on their leaves
for snoozing, as I do,
a book open at my heart,
in a lawn-chair
    on this new platform?
"Sturdy," says Larry.
    "It's not going anywhere."
Too sturdy for any foreseeable necessity,
which is my way.

Just a mystery,
    in which a man...
two women...
a dog as sentinel observer...
    Maybe the witty detective
can solve it, then go home.
    The book's now fallen to the platform
at the chair's side.
Maybe I'll wake up again, in rain.
All joy is temporary.

Fantasy baseball?
One might think of a man
    gone sour because youth was
a disappointed trip to the rained out game,
Marilyn's refusal,
    one of a few stinging nettles
still remembered.
He just can't get shed of that one.

The memory longs to forget, blah, blah,
    in this perfect day,

nothing to say.
He went south into Virginia,
   or was it North Carolina?
Was it indeed Marilyn?
  He can't find the itch. Lust, too,
is temporary. When will it get going
finally?

In the mystery,
the man takes a women,
  the dog watches, and the other woman
hears scratching
at the door foreshadowing confrontation.
Is it a guide dog?
  Somebody winds up dead,
and in the reading
I'm glad it isn't me.

   I've been that detective,
not quite as witty,
but in the end I go home too.
  You're just a few feet away,
in the kitchen, cooking up something.

   "What happened?
At the conclusion,
was there a satisfactory solution?"
There's a feather
  on the floor at your feet,
a clue, unaccounted for.
   "Yeah,
but the dog,
it still nettles.
I can't make much out of that."

## Hooked

Fish gotta swim, and pheasants
must rise from the fallow corn,
until fish get hooked

and shotgun opens, a crack
in the winter air. Now beginneth
the long night, period.

Yet connected to a source of power,
the clumsy ship off the coast
of Ireland, black night's water,

his hand at the tiller and the damaged
hooker on deck between them,
mate and captain, the only crew.

Over the waves, a distant beacon,
foreign hum in the dark engine: a story,
any story.

# Table

The table was a tree
before the men and machines
    got hold of it
and made it into something
unrecognizable, erasing its source
in history.

When the tree fell,
it sighed for the lost view
of opportunity,
    that weight in the top branches
in the wind
when the boy climbed
for a look at the outer world, the future,
or perhaps it was the boy sighing.

    There was in fact little to see
of interest to boys,
before girls, who made model airplanes
also with a source in wood.
This was a long time ago,
    when the world was younger.
It's an old piece of furniture.

I sit at the table, thinking possibly
of the tree, the boy, that view,
    all seemingly felt in the wood,
even through
the polyurethane finish
I have provided against stain.

But what is stain, a circle
    of sweat from an iced glass,

spill-over at surfeit,
imprint of the damp palm's signature,
any soaking down
        in search of the living sap,
which is no longer there?

The table is dead, the boy is dead,
    the view will never be seen again
from that exact vantage,
        even though he was probably thinking
of girls with no knowledge or specificity
and not really looking.
I, oddly, am still alive.

And the chair?
What passions do I release in this repose,
palms on the table, a hard chair, so I might avoid drifting
    into dangerous day-dreaming,
and yet I do anyway.

Gloriole, a nimbus
provided by sun through branches
    at the rot of a creek
where crawdads dwelt
and the tadpoles turned into minnows,
now an industrial complex of some sort,
    as much of the Midwest
as well as California
is laid waste.

You might have been Barbara,
or Jean, or Barbara-Jean,
        dope on my fingers
covering that other scent,
not of eucalyptus, that was later,

but the redolent pungency of uncleanliness
in childhood.
    The wood then
was the berry-vine, smoked not for pleasure
but imitation. Perhaps
        the adult can be a child again,
for loss there also was gain.
She took the crawdads home and cooked them,
mother attentive at her elbow.
And now the window.

Looking back up from arthritic knuckles
the wood frame holds,
    as a space through branches,
other trees, birds,
        a blond cat, sky-blue,
and the bay's waters
placid now, almost a mirror
after turmoil
    of storm marking the tail end
of a wintery spring.
New leaves obscure the feeder,
    weeds dip at the planters' lips,
the cat's pregnant.
There are clocks everywhere.

Foolish, then, was our decency,
a naivety considering only tomorrow
    or the next day as future,
a trip to the Pike
for magic of freaks and hot-dogs,
on our bikes, going
    just about anywhere, for comfort
of returning.

The last time I saw you crushes me,
your hands on my shoulders,
    sniffing the foolish bath of perfume,
just the image of you standing there
before falling away, as if
hacked from wood.

There may have been death
all around us. There was,
but we couldn't touch it, that future:
    sap dried up in the cripples,
failed surgeries, heart attacks,
and amputations.
    I remember only your hands
at the frame, looking in a me,
that adult posture
—your mother,
    your father going off to work?—,
but I'm not really trying.
    Wasn't there a eucalyptus tree,
*that* scent, redolent with death?
    It seems a little sinister now,
but only when I push it.
Perhaps the whole room is a tree,
but for the lamps, bed, and the carpet.

It's a long way from "my home town,"
one of many, and thus
    dozens of gestures of endings
as life goes on without you.

I just wanted to go back once again
for a moment,
but the tree now is a table.
    Only the dead seem stable,

palms pressed down on the surface.
    I can see for a good distance
through the window,
        tall trees in the future
at somebody's horizon
where the sap still resides.

## Prayer for Travelers
*— for Jean-Pierre & Aline Seeuws*

I pray now unto the gods of travel,
who are vessels
containing absence in the mind
and, in the body, anticipations of arrival,
who are gods only
in creation of ambivalence,
and to their witnesses,
      sedentary old men and old
women, who sit on benches in the square
watching comings and goings,
briskly in mornings, heads tilted
earthward at evening's exhausted
returnings
and witnessing those also
      arriving from other places,
this square and the buildings beyond it
a new place, and those leaving
lugging belongings
who will not be returning.

What is home? This square,
      these flowers, annual stink
of the ginkgo, a catch in the throat
at sound of the traveler's footsteps coming
from Houston? Paris?,
      business of busyness,
that dim light in the window
placed there only to welcome him
back again, a homecoming,
though everything seems temporary
in this uncertain America.

Embarrassment of wars and of patriots,
>   agony of children sent to die in places
where the children of those places are also dying,
frustrated rage at politicians
bent on traveling to town squares
for vacuous talking and at those sitting
complacently in offices, plotting
the permanent absence of others.
Where then is home
>   when houses fall down and even
squares disappear while travelers are away?

Let us pray then
in anticipation of this departure
and the arrival which is a homecoming,
as the light left behind is extinguished
along with these voice that say, stay, don't go.
Let the travelers return to the foreign
yet familiar, the stink of ginkgo faint
>   feeling in the nostrils,
that bark on the old trees, the ancient
city squares, the rediscovery
in the unpacking of forgotten belongings.
The scent of remembered flowers,
>   strange in their redolence,
will fade into the common after a day, a week,
until home reclaims them completely
and they can think once again
of those left behind,
in this sweet and uncertain America.

# Moon

Oh moon within my vacant gaze,
her figure turning vivid in memory
as if you were modern
and she celebrant of your lost innocence,
no matter they have played golf
upon your bland surface, not of trees,
rivers or pollutants.
She is guileless,
yet attendant to my needs
though I don't often see them.
Oh slice of moon, satellite, green cheese,
I beseech thee,
let this continue indefinitely
under your changing variety of signs.
Since I have found love,
what else is there?
These astronauts
have not really altered the view,
her figure turning, still vivid
under your glow in the memory.
That this could go on forever,
let it.

## Gardening

Behind things left in front,
under the faint yellow
light of a nightclub,
as if a drunkard in decay
hidden by fractured neon,
this grapefruit
dressed up for oblivion
in a fur of mold.

What else has been forgotten,
a light in the basement,
anniversary of the many heroes,
some sour appointment?

Having tried unsuccessfully
to keep trying, having
arrived at no understanding,
might have purchased a ticket
to exotic places,
then forgotten the pruning
of acquaintances and closer company.

Yet a blush on the green tomatoes,
the silvery eggplant in maturity
discovered behind leaves.

Clouds open like heavy curtains,
light of the morning sun.
What is ready is cut free.

# DEATH SENTENCES

*For Miriam*

*forever*

# Inspiration

The cat is out of the bag,
and the music is Bill Evans, not the trio,
but alone.

Somewhere along the line,
under the strains
    of *My Foolish Heart*,
the people in this room
are filled with ideas.

There is no room,
and there are no people.

This is my inspiration.
There is only Bill Evans.

# Standard-18,
## *There Will Never Be Another You*

How quickly does the weight of time come down upon us.
Foreclosure:
        Christmas, Passover, Independence,
and roses
wilting in the pot you may have placed for them,
the various frustrated markers.

And long gone too
the freshness of things discovered:
        the texture of your hair,
your beautiful toes,
my finger pressed in the wetness of your arm pit.

What is romance?
Outside
the winter wind is cautionary
snow flakes into wet drops on the window.
        Soon the shovel, the broom,
those thoughts of you while digging
in a daze.

And yet a chickadee, shivering on the feeder, alert,
his last dance
to music I had thought to cling to,
        Keith Jarrett's fingers in 'My Old Flame,'
as if the keys were lips,
            other songs, another fall,
maybe another spring.

Love is the answer:
        the gone ones answering
in the earth's ripening,

should spring
ever come to this troubled mind,
should the living forget those haunted
images of the dead,
so the dead might live in the common memory.

Last week, justice was in the offing.
I aimed to shoot the rabbit
but missed him.
      He had chewed at your flowers,
his nature.
Only in mistaken weaponry was he spared.

What is death?
      What is the nature
of these endings?
The flowers multiply before wilting
as do the rabbits.

Undeterred:
That waking dream
      of a delicate young man in glasses
in uniform, in boot camp, and the bastard
Chief Petty Officer
finding a bit of soap in one ear.
He removed it brutality with a pencil,
      then forced him into the shower
in his clothing, his glasses, in front of all of us.
He wept then, water soaking his uniform,
      mingling with tears on his dignified face.
He had lost the terms of his life.
He had lost his life.
Would that I was older then,
and had this rifle.

Nights like this:
I'll be standing there with someone new,
      threads of a silken scarf in memory in my fingers,
other lips that I might kiss.
Our thrill is gone.

Maudlin:
The books you gave me,
      many unread. Your various accomplishments
seen but unseen.

      And in our moment of parting
you were alone in the bed
six feet away.
You were always alone.

So much sabotage
      on our long road home:
women and drink, my failings, my insanity.
I would ask for a moment of forgiveness.
Too late. At the end
      you didn't know my name.
Who was I then?

There's a poem in here somewhere,
a kind of fiction that I remember
or imagine,
visiting Walter's farm.

Dinner and talk, fine wine,
      and in the morning
out in the yard, close to the silo,
with the shotgun.

"Too many pigeons."
        Doing something destructive?
I don't remember.

I raised the gun awkwardly
into the sky.
Three pigeons fell to the ground,
two dead, one
        struggling to leave this planet,
there
in the scatter of hay and straw.

"You have to kill her," Walter said.
"It's humane."

I couldn't do it. The passage
        would be her own,
as yours was.

That night I returned to the pigeon's resting place,
then went to my bed in the old farm house.
I slept the sleep of a wanderer.

About pigeons and rabbits, a guy in a shower,
a chickadee, the tassels on your hat,
a rifle and a shotgun.
        About life and death, about dreaming,
about the picture of you with your new bicycle,
about memory:
        the dead's messages
written into the skins of the living.

And the last story:

In the early morning,
        before the living rose up,
I carried you to the car,
        then drove to the cemetery.

The place was empty,
but for the birds,
        those mourning doves
you so loved.

And in the earth,
in front of the stone marker
upon which your name was carved,
        I dug a deep hole
and buried your ashes
among tree roots and stones.

You were not there.

## Death Sentences

1

Stumbled among stones until
toes wetted in surf's gentle wash
having come here to the edge
where pipers plow with pointed beaks
only to dash away
leaving momentary excavations
that pucker then disappear
as memory holes
in which past life might live
and die as all things possible
become nothing
here at the end of land
just inches beyond stones that were
Flint Granite Quartz and Glass.

2

Subdued danger of the brown-tale rash
and clothing for outside adventure
otherwise luxurious living
as days turn into years
and months are theatrical characters
whose presence is accusing every day
although unbidden
in this crucible that limps along
until the old man swallows up the young
and he who was a fraud and fake
discovers his flagrant character
too late for correction
out on the porch in perfect weather
where he sits and weeps.

3

What price vocabulary of the living world
few names for flowers trees and dogs
that bloom and move so certainly
until windy weather cars or saws possess them
lest they stay and become a prophecy
of what's to come
days without end of gorgeous weather
which the moved along will not savor
here in the pleasure of trials and tribulations
as the mystery train travels
into uncertain futures
and even the sick at heart
look out the window to see
rows of lilacs and coreopsis blooming.


4

In Truro when the time was ripe
which is a metaphor
including all passengers
even those blinded by ambition
there was a house set against storm
in which a woman once lived
then died leaving parcels of her life behind
in bags that relatives sorted
in preparation for a yard sale
of worn cutlery and dishes
dresses and furniture
and jewelry impressed with her scent
who had lived in the way we all live
and will leave in the same way too.

5

Back to the sea
where they fish in sunset
and never see it for what it is
clock of the earth's turning
a possible message
for those facing into the glow
who are struck blind when they turn
until their world comes into focus
transient and then fixed
for the time being
all this before the inevitability beckons
and legs start failing
even when standing still while fishing
hauling up dark bottom dwellers.


6

They who are here are no longer here
yet those who are gone
are still truculent after passage
into cocoons in memory's storage
where light footed and dancing
they break through that webbing
and after hours of drinking
in fake celebration
do the living stumble intoxicated
into their beds and the nightly
death sleep which presages
until they rise up in the morning
the rot of night in their nostrils
empty of memory.

7

Much of the dark preaching goes unnoticed
by the fidgeting children
pew locked and longing
before the sepulcher teaching and the threats
while those who know better are praying
for the eternal
that is already there
outside these confines
in trees and sun and ever changing grasses
beside the concrete parking lot and the cars
that will in time
enter the living earth
as will all people and this steeple
when preaching is forgotten.


8

Back to the sea again those gentle swells
upon which gulls sit
and wreckage washes up to be examined
so that the distant past might live again
in reconstructions of the sailors' mess
a wheel house and old coins
whose value is found in imprints
of kings and monarchs from foreign places
that no longer exist
but in the fascination for a cleansing
by retrogression that will turn the clocks back
and the dead will become the living
though in the same frustrations
that the living now inhabit.

9

X my only love
harken back to sea wrack
in childhood on these beaches
where plovers still run and fishermen
cast out their plugs that search
in deep waters for a kind of offering
so that families might devour the sacraments
brought up
and you left the table
hungry for ice cream
melting into death on your fingers
and all your friend are running forward
or away as sun sinks
and the moon rises.


10

A story in which there are no characters
but for the sun's wash on everything
that is not human
but can act that way in yucca
dipping its long spear as if nodding
and the small nest the snake approaches
with an attention
humans might mimic in metaphor
seeing the world from the ground up
to avoid the dying pines and oaks
that will in time fall away
as what is now becomes a desert
and all that seemed possible has its ending
here there or anywhere.

11

When at times our Sunday best is not enough
and guarded under raiments
of personality we go unnoticed
at church banquets and dancing frenzy
in order to find a presentation of the living
where constant motion forestalls the peaceful ending
that dark promise
and as clothing wears and we under it
find resignation of peaceful stillness
in which solitude in vacant eyes
might understand the final closure
banishing ego
until in that unexpected rattle
everything is left behind for the others.


12

Another story of a man this time
who in the metaphor is less than a stick figure
though bound over for autopsy
in a well lighted room
smelling of gentle chemicals
while relatives upstairs are waiting
to see him as he was in life
and all in the vibrant world
speak the uniqueness of this passage
yet doors stand open
beyond which their endings beckon
even as the deliriums of action
deny its inevitable coming and the flowers
around the casket begin to stink.

13

Ah yes the flowers the trees the birds
and the sea under which and above
uncounted time keeps passing
leaving the dead behind and forgotten
until there is none left for memory
though not yet not yet
for the fishermen still face the sea
and Caroline remains lascivious there
awaiting upon a satisfaction
that as with all else is transitory
while fish hang dead on the line
and birds fly into glass
blocking a passage
similar to the ones we think protect us.


14

Having come now to an ending
though not the end
that has no future beginnings
even in bacteria
that float unseen on the waves' surface
and presages nothing
in a journey on that sea always returned to
as if it were some message
speaking of life's continuance eternally
above remnants of a sunken past forgotten
when what is remembered
has no living vessel to contain it
even death becomes silent
and tongues are rotten in the mouth.

# The Red Ribbon

1

The red ribbon is tied in her hair,
and it celebrates her hair,
blond, a quarter inch of black at the roots,
and she thinks of the President's madness
and that quarter inch
of the real emerging. What can she do?
He waits at the edge of the wood, and she
in her plain country shift
is ready to get rid of all thoughts of
presidents and houses and senates,
since her head is filled with congress,
and the tales of the red ribbon
are bouncing as she moves quickly toward him
in the failing light.

2

Everybody fancies the ribbon,
it's red with gold thread
    stitched in along its borders
and there's an emblem.
Perhaps the rich will conspire,
anything to get it.
Yet it is only a ribbon and not currency
though that is the way the rich see it.
Money, money, money,
    there's nothing like it!
It's only a ribbon, and yet
it is beautiful and not precious,
but like the man said, "Business is business,
but love is bullshit."

3

The document is closed with a red ribbon
that the President struggles to untie,
then he gets it
and all in the small audience applaud.
With a flourish, he signs it
    then holds it up
turning as if it were some holy text.
Then all applaud again.
Birds chirp in the White House trees.
Chipmunks settle down
    in holes in the lawn.
Who is the first lady?
The only thing in the room
that seem real is the red ribbon.

4

She gave him a red ribbon
that he didn't want,
then insisted that he snake it
    through his belt loops
and tie it in the front.
This was just the beginning,
for she was foolish and insistent,
and he was her sap.
Ribbons are without power
to hold pants up,
thus does he dance away
covering his crotch.
She wont quit.
It's *her* ribbon. He's *hers*.

5

The red ribbon is torn from the gift
of the unknown anticipated
by the one who leans forward
a flower in her hair
wondering what it could be
as the giver sweats in his own anticipation:
will she like it, will she demure?
Does it matter what the box contains?
Some say it's the thought that counts.
She is not thinking, but wishing
to like anything given by him.
There's a good deal of hesitation.
Open the damned box!
She toys with the ribbon.

6

The red ribbon is only a ribbon
until it stands for something:
    solidarity, the battle against disease,
blood of course and even stroke.
The red ribbon has no power,
yet it is powerful when worn be people
in certain groups, even by those
not on the barricades, but in offices,
    writing changes to various regulations,
the backbone of movements.
The official sits at his desk.
He is assaulted by paper, and the red ribbon
    dances on the heads
of the thousands
gathered for change.

# Flowers

## 1 New Guinea Impatiens

I wonder if in New Guinea they are impatient,
as we are: all those languages, sharp and melodious,
on the streets of Los Angeles, and tribes conversing
in Mount Hagen and the Gulf villages.
     Impatient for roasted pig, dance costumes,
the Singing Dog. Impatient for a change in scenery,
a trip at least to Bakersfield,
a different life.

Flowers ring our East Coast properties
and are not there by happenstance.
     Each choosing, each careful planting,
each impatient for its blooming.

The times are hard in Massachusetts, New York City,
as they might well be in New Guinea and Los Angeles,
and yet there is certainly dancing and singing, each song
a flower
parceled out in a new beginning.

I will press my face into their moist blossoming.
All our flowers, as well as those in New Guinea,
are sexual.

Henceforth, I will be singing and will not be impatient.
These flowers were purchased
for what seems now
a song.

## 2  Tulip Feeder

Humming birds on the glass feeder
shaped like a tulip.
    They suck up the nectar,
and spill drops of sugar

        on the grass below, the flowers below,
the worm below, and the chipmunk:
all there or coming there
for nourishment.

Now suddenly do we discover
the snake
    in this polluted grass,
who climbs the pole after a mouth full.

Humming birds are fragile.
Thus are they swift, and only
vulnerable at rest,
but for the hawk's
death strike.

This tulip is made of glass
and will not grow old and die,
as the real tulips will.

These humming birds will grow old and die,
as will this grass, the chipmunk,
the snake.

Below this atmosphere, the polluted earth.
It too might die, as will we,
eventually. The worm will search and find us all
and is immortal.

## 3 Lantana

Haunted lantana
unpruned, your green vines
      reaching out for another place,
a life
in which your star clusters-
yellow, purple, red, bandana cherry
and Carlos, golden Christine
      and violet—
are properly tended by someone
other than me,

      that one in winter, the lazy bum,
who has left you there to wither
into skeleton grey stalks
      as in movies or paintings where,
unbeknownst to the heroine,
fairies dance among rot
near a marsh in England.

I have no time for flowers,
and they have little time for me.

Yet your beauty is remarked,
if only in passing,
      when you reach to touch
my starboard leg
your radiation blossoms rustbit
for lack of water.

And so I water you and wait
for cherry sunrise to return again.

## 4  A Rose

Who gives a rose with care for satisfaction,
but pathetically, a single stem, denuded
of its guarding thorns,
lest they prick the lover's palm,
his could be the stupid music of a love
for she who sticks it in a narrow fluted vase
and thus forgets it, until
she hears a knocking at the door
and thinks "it's him,
come for some reward"
that will not be given,
but for an enigmatic smile,
and "thank you for that lovely flower"
that in the meantime has blossomed,
then faded
and dropped its fleshy red petals
to form a sad circle on the glass table
out of sight.

## 5  Funereal Flowers

Nobody should lie among gladiolus, standing
     in tall wicker at the quilting of his new home.
Character, moral integrity, sayeth the florist
garnering wealth.

Yet the mourners admire them, and the white lilies
     [innocence restored to the departed soul]
and the red roses [grief and sorrow, and courage too].
         And their various scents, blossoming, pollen
and lantana, and the memory of bees buzzing and sucking nectar.
They cannot see the dead from their seats.

All summer long, chrysanthemums [death
and grieving] and white carnations.
All these signature values imagined by florists.

The bride stands at the window.

Where is the flower girl, the ring bearer?
Where is the groom?
Yet this is a marriage of worlds
and the transit between them,
and flowers stir in the breeze
provided by the air conditioner.

No one is at peace in his casket,
his new home.
Memories of childhood, of wild flowers
presented to his bride at a similar altar,
memories of last week,
all gone, but for the transit.

Before the lid closes,
before the bearers move to their stations,
before the florist counts his money,
      and before the staged ceremony comes
to it's theatrical end,
the dead shall rise up from his casket,
and his body
or at least his soul, or in the imagination,
shall walk out into the summer sunset,
followed by the scent of flowers.

## 6 The Wrist Corsage, A Memory

Brilliant pink cloth flowers,
feathered wrist corsage,
fancy in its old conservative way.

It's the homecoming dance,
pink carnations
in a little white box
held awkwardly at his hip.

"Here," he says
and hands it over,
in memory.

She's forgotten his tie,
his awkward smile,
his father's car.

Once upon a time,
long gone.

She thinks of the little box,
his crisp white cuff,
that awkwardness in the dancing.

She's forgotten his name, yet remembers
that fleeting kiss,
his lack of imagination with flowers.


## 7 The Yellow Chalice Vine

"Let's go to college," Ollie said.
Corpus Christi, the navy,

1960,
        but I was thinking of Mary Grace
naked in the placid surf,
            flowers in her hair,
though on the Gulf the Portuguese man-of-war
were drifting in.

"Why not," I said,
      our thoughts drifting too,
heading for California.

Two young guys,
no real passions in our eyes,
        but wonderment of where to go,
           what to do.
We should make plans, I thought,
but there, again, was Mary Grace.

A late fall afternoon on Padre Island,
      almost empty in those days,
we walked along the beach,
then headed inland
            —low, gentle, dunes—
and came upon a stand of pine,
a little forest here
      in Texas,
—only sixty yards square—
where we had spent a year and more
without sufficiency,
         but for those flowers
in the women's hair
we thought to love
and leave.

I had not seen the character in trees.
I was bewildered,
    always looking inward,
but these branches were skirts
falling over one another,
    long green candle fingers
hung from hidden hands,
close to brushing the sandy ground.

Then came upon a small clearing in this fiction
and discovered the trunk
    of a dead tree, severed
to a small man's height
    and slightly leaning
under the encircling weight of the Chalice Vine,
its glossy foliage
and its aphrodisiac flowers, large yellow petals
    curling back and changing
to become bright gold in their opening.

This is the tree of the wind, Kieli,
    god of the wind and black magic.

Thick vines encircled the body of the dead tree,
snaked under arms,
between legs,
    stroking a cheek, a neck,
all hidden beneath the foliage of vines and leaves.
A flower had opened near the leaning tree's head.
Its petals brushed the bark, his shadowy face.

The Chalice Vine is erotic,
its embrace the embrace of sexual love,
    but also love itself in sex
and also life.

I thought I saw the dead tree shudder
in the vague scent of coconut.

"Let's go to college."
Ollie spoke in a laughing whisper,
breaking the spell.

We turned away.

The flowers seemed to be watching us,
burning their presence
into the backs of our heads.

These were the Cups of Gold.


## 8 Pansies

They call you a pansy,
and I, for one, am watching
your delicate movements,
      dancing around the field,
never footing the ball
or the other players.

Pansies: the color in the core,
      shape of an eagle landing,
a hairy old man's face,
as in a coven,
a crowd of dogs watching.

The field is surrounded
      by pansies, a rainbow,
and the pink rosie posies
stand among them, on long green stems.

And you, my dear child,
are moving
within that encircling.
    It's only a game after all,
these laughing insults.

And at the intermission,
or the time out, or at half time,
    you are prancing, smiling,
as you move to the sideline,
a pansy.

It doesn't matter to me
if you are a boy
or a girl.


## 9  Oldfield Toadflax

Skinny as you are with your blue hats
I love you,

which to some may well be a sin,
give gay marriage
and the domino effect:

marriage to cats and chickens, to a gold fish,
a sparrow hawk, a brother,
and of course dogs and hogs.

But flowers are not such fools,
their beauty your beauty,
that of feral, vegetative music.

Some call you a weed even in
your blooming.
Yet you are gay, swaying,
nodding in the breeze.


10 That Begonia

The big oak is dropping its acorns
that ping among withered leaves on the little deck
Larry and I constructed
long ago,
       which time is,
in the way of years,
gone now, here in the early fall in North Truro.

Nothing much:
these skeletal trees, these clapboards
turning grey, this world of no distinguishing color.

And yet, in a brown ceramic pot at the deck's edge,
       the bright red Switzerland begonia,
its waxen, veined and pointed green leaves
there to dress that blooming,
           flowers whose petals fold and gather
into a tight fleshy center
that seems almost edible,
as red as any bloody satisfaction.

We round the house
and set out on the narrow road
that runs between endless fields
of withered corn, their last cobs fallen,
as they soon will, as far as the eye can see.

Abandoned cars in weeds at the road side,
         rusted and burned out.
Flowers that thrived in passenger seats
are wilted now.
             The sky is dark, heavy black clouds
full of cold rain.
We hear the quiet moan of a few mourning doves,
invisible among the stalks.

This is not Truro,
or anywhere, though it too seems lifeless.

As fall comes on,
I've been thinking about my life,
my losses,
my lover and my friends.
And I've been thinking too about that begonia.

It was so red!


## 11  Still Life with Geranium

A dead duck, a ham sandwich, a trout,
         and to the left a dim candle.
On the far right,
a rifle, a fishing pole.

In the center all is uncertain,
as are the passing days,
         but for this uncommon geranium,
the order of a singular flowering,
limp, purple petals,
black business at the core.

The duck will not fade away.
        The sandwich will not be eaten.
The trout will not decay.

But the geranium, like all flowers,
will bow to the inevitable
leaving the center of the still life vacant.


## 12 Flower Children

Puberty will not harm them.
        Sex will not harm them.
The State will not prevail against them.
Harmony will protect them.

Tellytubbies'
        heads bristling with clover,
sunflowers, lavender, mushrooms,
even miniature pine trees,
cherries.

They will be dancing,
the youth of a nation comes forward,
        harmless, in subtle revolt.
The innocence of childhood is within them.
All will be well.

Flower Children
walking the streets of Beijing,
        teenagers, some a little older,
some shy.
Even in the rain, in humidity, in storm,
        no appeasement, luxury, no aggression.
They are crowned, casual.

They pace the earth, which is sidewalks,
streets, school halls, parks.

I saw them from a dark doorway and laughed,
and they laughed too, then spoke to one another,
     looked into shop windows, bodegas,
mirrors.
Flowers were growing from their heads.

Maturity will not harm them.
     Singularity will not harm them.
The state will not prevail against them.
Harmony will protect them.

"Let one hundred flowers bloom!"

# I Don't Know

1

Shovels scrape on the sidewalks
while it's still snowing
        and wind is blowing the drifts
back over the cleared spaces
to again institute that silence provided
in winter when snowy weather
covers all the sins of frustrated cracked streets
that are evidence of a government
without will or money
and I don't know
what to make of my life these days
when care is delivered
        in mail and recorded phone calls
without a human face.

2

Don't mean to be silly
        when care is delivered
up in the voice of a woman who says
I'm Inder then bla bla
may I help you then helps you
        so you see while on hold
the way the sun throws lacy shadows
on that massive building that sits back
over the cleared spaces
        that once housed workers
and machines and progress but
I don't know
because there is the sun
and Inder saying may I help you.

3

The way the sun throws lacy shadows
through the trees and dresses up my dress
with geometric patterns
      I can't read is the point actually
though I can see
the eyes of men standing
around looking at me
and can read the future
in which the looking becomes mutual
and respectful and
      I don't know
but that a purchase on the real life
so you see while on hold
there is no other important goal
and won't give it more time.


4

Swim suits that look like saucy underwear
and men outfitted in skimpy shorts
with geometric patters
and pockets
as protection for their delicates
lest they become an embarrassment
of a kind never examined
and won't give it more time
      so that I don't know
what to make of a life spent
in attraction on beaches in nothing
but exotic clothing
and wishes for romantic adventure
while gulls mate at the shore.

5

So that a voice speaks out of places
that are sea churned or forest enabled
      or maybe in recognition
of a kind never examined
that there is only place
and pockets
of talk in a real world
since I don't know
about ideas floated on nature's absence
      in the way of desire unspecified
for she who is created by the one
who imagines her figure in garments
applied like those on a paper doll
and I know about that.


6

In the way of desire unspecified
the dance keeps yearning for the dancers
      as does the empty orchestra its fiddles
or maybe it's recognition
that nothing can begin
until those with faces in phones
put down everything
and see a world beyond the ego's hold
or it could be
that nothing can be done for them
but I don't know that's true
      because the light behind their eyes
will look out in spite of them
and all will be bright in their world.

7

Or it could be
that revelers beyond their vision
      are engaged in frivolous activities as
the dance keeps yearning for the dancers
and I don't know exactly what's happening
though I do understand
that something comes next
      as did the lindy the tango and disco
but of course that doesn't say it all
for time's shadow lingers
each time the possibility threatens them
with the world
and someday not too far away
it will be skeletons dancing.


8

To the right are the believers
and to the left those locked into engagement
with the world
      though troubled in ignorance
of calculations I don't know much about
when it comes to a haunting awareness
that something comes next
for all who live on the edge
of governments and their understandings
about everything that alludes them
      as they prelude coming disaster
while those on the right believe them
and to the left is continuing fear
of the rolling thunder.

9

For all who live on the edge
where the township is not managed
 theirs is poverty and freedom
from the daily babble and yet
I don't know
of their understandings
about everything that alludes them
for to be among the privileged
and thus ignorant
is solace
at the edge of somnambulism
where everything seems vaguely possible
as when the moon rises
and the magic carpet carries them away.


10

My underwear is vacant now
and that which was the lurid prize
 for everyman
is solace
as when the moon rises
and I squat upon the beach
to drain my yellow offering like any animal
but I don't know except in sisterhood
will the hammer come down on those others
who in their ignorance
have sinned without know it
 sorrow in the judgment for them
since the hammer is for those
in power and indiscriminate lust.

11

The butcher cuts the meat
that bleeds upon the block
and is presented to the everyman
      for promised satiation
and that which was the lurid prize
so almost sacristan is eaten by those
who in their ignorance
      are smart and sophisticated
though I don't know
since smart is a dime a dozen
but understanding
is the coin of the year
and there is little enough of that
to fill a thimble a shot glass or an wink.


12

The years might limp along
without much understanding
      of the fly on the wall
but understanding
is a record of defeats yet
I don't know
since there is sunshine on the wall
and there is little enough of that
when the fly departs
      her absence in memory
that she is still there
as everything stops for a moment
and those who have departed are back
again under the sun.

13

Outside where I have planted
this woman's mystery garden
      as everything stops for a moment
and I don't know
if the flowers with sister names
who are Rose Jasmine and Lily
will bloom
as much as their namesakes
      in a troubled time
without much understanding
so that a nosegay perched upon my head
is given back as reckoning
and old clothing is worn in the gardening
by those who will alter the world.


14

To again institute that silence provided
so that you see while on hold
      and can read the future
of a kind never examined
that there is only place
or maybe it's recognition
that something comes next
      for all who live on the edge
of their understanding
who in their ignorance
are smart and sophisticated
and those who have departed are back
as everything stops for a moment
and this I know.

## After the Storm

They open their coats to reveal
school clothing business attire palates
pajama tops and a women dressed
for an evening out
while those in the wrong shoes
step carefully to avoid the slush
and an old woman my age
is approached by a young man
who lends her his aid
and they limp arm in arm
to the curb.
The storm is over
and all are moving with purpose
heading for imagined adventures.

## After the Photograph

Who will have my picture standing
upon art deco
like the one of my parents,
she with a tennis racket along
her shapely leg, he so young yet
presaging his early death?

       She never played that game,
he bit the dust at forty-three,
and I still alive
for the time being at least.

Will the photograph speak to someone
as this one does to me?
Will the sun cast shadows
across my face also?

Young lovers comfortable
in the promise of their futures.
Who might gaze at them and wonder?

## After the Concert

Light jackets, silk frocks.
It's spring, late evening.

Couples talk about dinner,
edging those who are fooling around,
laughing and kissing.
      Talk mummers, shoes scrape
on concrete. That's all.

Colored lights
in the buildings across the way.
It has rained,
and the streets glisten.

A plane passes high over head,
and below it
they can hear the distant hum.
It sounds like music.

## After Long Silence

Birds chatter and speak to one another
in the park in the night
where small animals are free
of the human condition and can move
out of hiding. All this
while I sleep in the quiet house
and laughter and serious talk
is a ghost all the way to breakfast
after which peace is forgotten
and the energy of the day
speaks out in useless palaver
for ears that have awakened
to begin it all once again.

## After the Wedding

The bridesmaids gather together
in a clutch of inward attention, tall and slim,
imagining their futures,
and I find myself lusting for each of them
      which is not a wise thing to be saying
or thinking these days.

So I sidle up to the bride
as if in my presence I can be forgiven,
and the bridegrooms part awkwardly
in their nervousness an ill fitting tuxedos.

"Best wishes," I say, and to the groom
"Congratulations,"
these proper salutations.

There's shrimp on thin sticks, goat cheese,
prosciutto wrapped persimmons,

      and there I am,
lonely for my wife
and our ceremony
as the band plays *I remember you.*

# After the Fall

A man on a ladder
that disappears into the clouds.

He looks like a child
at this distance.

Then he reaches the clouds
and enters them.

We can barely see him,
but we see him.

Then comes the decision.
Will he look up and search the sky

for the future, or will he look down
into the vibrant present?

Then he falls.

# After Divorce

Two sad sacks,
he with his hands stuck deep in his pockets,
        it's winter, she
in the mink that was his present
twenty years ago.

What should they do,
find another, glory in freedom,
go after that "Self Realization" scam?

The kids were long gone.
        They'd both felt "in a rut,"
and each of them had taken up,
briefly, with another.

Twenty-five years of habits
carved in the brain,
those beautiful children,
a few moments of understanding.

Watch them.
He wears a new suit that doesn't
quite fit, and his mind is always elsewhere.
She's sold her mink, has lost weight,
and is now skinny.

Both are hunched over slightly,
standing or walking.

## After Angelica Waiting

She is dressed in her Saturday best
and a little extra in anticipation:
    a few ruffles, possibly ludicrous
given her age.
She's had her hair done, blonde,
and it sparkles.

In restaurants four times
and once for a long walk in the city.
He's a little late;
he never is.

Children in the park across the way,
their grace, their certainty
    in losing time,
as her mind drifts away to other things,
her life, her dead husband

    —and then it's much later,
no more children,
all the stores have closed,
a dark quietness.

She left long ago.

## After Longstanding

There was music
having existed or continued
for a long time.
Showers might have fallen on the party,
his retirement, so that
were he to weep at the loss
of everything,
the violins might rise in the strains
of *Some Enchanted Evening.*
But he is dignified
where he stands toying
with his brand-new watch.
He smiles. He is gracious.
His severance check is in his pocket.

## After Lingering Illness

It's a summer day
    a few high clouds
soften the sun
that dresses the street
while trees filter and lay thin
shadow ribbons over the houses
mail boxes and cracked sidewalks
as birds sing
and porches hold swings sliders
chairs and tables
each house facing the street
and at number 42
a woman moves quickly down the steps
    into the warm sun
shedding her sick room garments
that fall and ripple
on the bushes and the grass behind her,
as shadow ribbons drape her fresh new body.

# After Death

Will there be vapors?
I think I can see through them.

There's a lunch counter,
my wife leaning against it

her figure glimmering white.
I can't stand the longing.

We move toward each other
slowly, stepping through clouds.

How soon might we touch?
The distance between us lengthens,

we're in a movie.
Then there's a fade out

into the final darkness.

## Afterwards

We could roll around for a while
then go out and lie naked
on cushions under the bird feeders
      to receive the small offerings
of chickadees and gold finches
that stain our chest with colorful
little dots.

Or maybe we could go out to dinner
and stare at each other lasciviously
across the table.

I might rise and kiss you
in front of everyone.
You might like that.

## I've Lost My Whistle

No longer can I call down my birds
or speak Bird.
It's a good thing I have no dog.

A woman stands
      in front of a pet-store window.
There are dogs inside.
Her strident whistle is a siren,
      and the dogs all rush to the window
and press their muzzles against it.

For a taxi, while cooking or idling,
for those dogs. For a beautiful woman passing
      (though I have never done that; well, once).
On your birthday, before dancing, to the sound of singing,
      tune of selling old clothing from a cart.
Of the knife sharpener,
the butcher,
while waiting for the dough to rise.
And of my father, calling us home
      from a night of kick-the-can,
in 1945.

A young man comes down the street whistling a tune
      from the American Song Book,
half forgotten.
*I Remember You.* He's lost
      in the complicated chord changes,
          and by the time he reaches me
it's a glorious confusion,
very much like Coltrane.

A bartender, a bell-hop, another taxi,
while you work, wetting it,
    Dixie, to start the game,
in the dark, blowing it on some corporate criminal, of a train,
       after love, past the graveyard,
          among ancient ruins,
answering the placid sea.

It's all gone.
I'm an old man counting his losses.
I can no longer accompany their going
with a tune.

## Disturbed

1

The genesis of all that rocks the waves
so that the character of flotsam in their curls
when found at surf side
is examined in curiosity and not wonder
    becoming the way of it
those lost chances for the vision
that precedes understanding
so that light coughing in public galleries
where quiet background music is Chopin
while a fog in the civilized head
calls for quiet appreciations
as turbulent oceans on canvases
in elaborate frames
hide their genesis.

2

He remembers the house on the hill
where quiet background music is Chopin
and he is once again in shorts and halter
while mother touches his brow
over and over again
so that he shivers in pleasure and the annoyance
that precedes understanding
as food turns foul in the mouth
where a boy stands in pajamas
ready for bed and aloneness
but for his chicken and rabbit
while the bell in the toy church
rings out death
over and over again.

3

The sea-side marshes are flooded
over and over again
as the oceans deposit their ships' wealth
among weeds and flowers
where fish now struggle in fresh water
and sunset rings out death in the voices
of remaining gulls
who head for their meals or nesting
while among the living
the dead rise up accusingly in memory
in night's shadows in lamp light
and guilt foolishly comes to roost
as food turns foul in the mouth
of those who feed upon death.

4

But now the mother is dead
and he is forty-three
in night's shadows in lamp light
whereupon a table holds his whiskey
that he might be oiled for reading
these books of those who feed upon death
in a history before his own
while among the living
politics rages
and there is no power in those
caught up in the maelstrom
as the dead rock in somebody's paradise
while hell is only a vague promise in books
as he raises his glass.

5

Caught up in the maelstrom
and white clouds hung low
over the bay's unshadowed majesty
the bait fish rose turbulent to the surface
in futile escape from the death below
while gulls squawked in the air
announcing death's presence
a feast for the fishermen who
      in this sad half natural cycle
gathered on waves in aggressive circles
again and again in view
of that house on the hill now vacant
as the sea held sway as witness
in a history before his own.

6

In futile escape from the death below
there are turbulent explorations
      and wet hair under his arms
in Chet Baker's honey in the living-room
where there are surf-stones
numbered and dated
in artistic piles that are sea tossed
and a messy abstract hung on the wall
in this sad half natural cycle
their juicy pleasures
and he knows she has him
      locked away from his taste
as clay animals strut on the mantle
and a shorn Poodle licks away at his toes.

7

Numbered and dated
the ships march out across the Atlantic
invisible beyond sight from the yearning shore
where there are surf-stones
and the mysteries inside the ships
are sea tossed
and mystery is memory
as much as the shuffling cargo
is scuttling towards its own future
while this drama's story
might reach out and touch the ships
even as the sea-side watchers
picnic or lie in the sun
and take delight in the empty waves.

8

This is about a man who returns
to the beach of his childhood at sixty-seven
where there are numbered stones
    scattered in the sand
and the vacant house on the hill
is the dead past
and about a confusion of papers
on a desk where he spends his life
in the construction of other lives
    so that all else becomes illusion
and he might think of the grave yard
as he imagines his mother
in the house on the hill above
gazing at the sea through windows.

9

And behind his mother's face
is the face of the wife that has joined her
so that all else becomes illusion
as he whittles away at the days
a glass of bourbon
among the scatter of papers on the desk
where time meanders
in the construction of other lives
while the body confronts its slow collapse
and he can hardly rise to reach his pencil
though he is strong enough
to confront his reading
and the confusion of dead characters
in the book beside the bourbon.

10

And in the book a man travels
into various tortured circumstances
    sets off to sail upon a distant sea
and discovers the rotting cargo
where time meanders
while paragraphs are both repeated
and created in his mind
at the edge of sleep
so that all else becomes illusion
and the cargo in his head
becomes the story
of loss and pathological longing
that lingers in the sleeper's imagination
as the book ridicules the reader.

## 11

And yet he is forced to the stories
that he has created
and the ones still to be brought
to a kind of life that is not life
though in time there will be an ending
and the cargo in the head will rot
as the story teller becomes the story
of loss and pathological longing
but for the bourbon
that sits among papers
and brings an appropriate dullness
to the one who is dealing in machination
as the desk is facing the window
through which the sea is unconcerned.

## 12

Once again the sea confronts the story
with disregard
as the sailor unfurls his canvas
upon which no words are written
and the bluefish school
at the ankles of the oyster picker
and the surf licks the toes
of the beautiful maidens
while far out and beyond vision
whales breach and blow
in those hours of the day
when the sea is placid
and holds their massive bodies
gently caressing them.

13

And so does he come to be eighty
and becomes the story
of a teller of limited ability
who nevertheless tells his stories
here on the Cape in May and sunlight
    where silence is a reminder
that the time is short
and all the while I am leaving
my bed at 4 a.m.
drinking coffee and remembering
that I love that past
in which I meet my people once again
admire their power in the memory
and write about them.


14

The sea is calm tonight
as seen from his window
and there are soft lights in fog
in the town out at the hook
    and people might be dancing there
or sitting at restaurant table
overlooking the placid waters
while house lights blink
along the curve of shore
and motors on the highway are trivial
as the fenders are still
at the gunwales of boats at the dock
yet the distance between us as always
is the wild uninterested sea.

## A Wink and a Nod

A hundred days of solitude
and you
      in memory standing
in your thoughtful beauty
at the bed side
even as my teeth fall out
and there's macular degeneration.
      I'm not really complaining,
just thought I'd mention it.

These rooms hold the desire
not the objects in them
but pathways
      where we followed or led one another
where we pulled out our chairs for dinner
and sat down facing each other
in the sinking sun.

      And I'm touching the walls
the handles on the kitchen cabinets
the pathway leading to the glass table
its smooth beveled edge
and dusty surface.

Solitude is not aloneness.
      There you are,
and I've been thinking about our adventure
at the gym.

You were sweating. Even your hair was soaked. You lifted for ten minutes more, grunting and gasping, then you dropped the bar with a thud, and we went home.

This didn't happen of course,
this imagining from remembered gestures,
and maybe it's a silly little joke.
      But we were silly, sometimes,
and we joked about a lot of things.
You were not powerful in your body.
It was your mind, your humor,
and my passion for them.

Sit down. Have a drink.
Be here.

I have your pictures, eternal
as these memories
haunt, yet sometimes please,
and you lost the car keys near the end.

      Our passages are worn into the rugs.
I might have winked at you at the gym.
You might have nodded in response.

A hundred ghosts, a half century.
Soon I too
go down.

# Child Lost in the Forest

1

She is dressed in shorts
and a blouse
      inappropriate
here among the shadows
cast down from dark trees.

It's late afternoon
and she is eight years old
and a little cold.

Where is my mother she whispers
her chin sunk into ruffles
at her throat.

She has been lost for a whole day.
What can she do?

Her hair is blond and long
and it falls to her shoulders
in golden ringlets.


2

The first night she slept
in a bed made of fallen pine boughs.
They were itchy and she was cold.

She was hungry.
The red berries on the bushes

were bitter and she spat them out,
and she didn't trust the mushrooms.

It is midday
and she is still wandering around
      looking for something to do.
Her bed is made
and she has found a stump for a seat.

She would wander off
      in search of a way back
to somewhere
but she fears losing the world
she now inhabits.

Look at her,
eight years old, thin
as a stick.

3

What happens now?
      The sun is sinking and she knows
she'll be staying there for another night.
          "Helga!" they'll call out,
seeing her, or hearing her,
as they emerge from the trees.

But that's latter.
She's hungry
and she must find food.

She searches the woods close by
and comes upon amaranth.

Her pink blouse is soiled,
      her white tennis shoes,
her shorts.
There are scratches on her bare legs.
She doesn't care.

She lays her foods out
      on the tall stump,
asparagus to the left, amaranth on the right
and chicory flowers for a garnish.

      It looks like a proper lunch,
and she jabs at the food with a sharp stick,
but its evening now
and the shadows turn her stump
into a table in a nightclub.

She better eat, then get to bed.
Animals are beginning to sound off.


4

She wakes in the morning
eats fireweed
      then pees among the trees.
Then she goes to her pine bed
and arranged the boughs so they look right.
She takes her place on the stump.

They come,
her stern father from the left,
dressed in conventional woods-wear,
      her mother clomping in from the right.
And her dour sisters and brother

and those from the village
enlisted for the search.

Her family stands to the side
while others laugh and chatter.
      And there are cameras and phones
and hand movies being made.

And there she is
      on her stump
among streamers and flags and dancers,
and she lifts the edge of her shorts
and slices her thin leg
with the sharp stick.

The last rays of the sun
wash geometric figures through her hair
and on her face and soiled blouse.
Blood drips from the wound.

Alone
in the maelstrom.

# Etudes —*for Miriam, in memory*

1

The impressions of bodies in the chairs
and couches in the living room
the scent of them absent
    while the land seen through
the window and the sea
remain constant
as your face in shadow
lingers to the sides of faces
I talk to smiling
unaware
yet sure in the third Irish and water
your face my compass
as conversation rots in the mouth
until the party's over.

2

Unaccounted for at sunset's prelude
in the window and the sea
beyond which night Paris still glimmers
    in our absence
in memory at least walking at the *Seine's* side
gazing at those who are young
as we grow older
and I am left only with thoughts
    of you buying *saucisson sec*
a *baguette* and wine for a picnic
the four of us together on grass in a park
who are now only one
    this self without lover and friends
as conversation rots in the mouth.

3

After a night of calm adventure
      monopoly and marijuana
the house in which we lived
container of a past was
in our absence
locked tight in memory
and I am left only with thoughts
of passion's last meal
      as you began to drift away
and for a while I was with you
lagging behind
summer fall and the last winter
in which you called me your father
mother and good friend.

4

Each day the breath of winter's sadness
locked tight in memory
of the last turkey you could not see
      as I forced your vision
hopelessly
while winter fell in crystal snow
lagging behind
the very thought of you twisted
until I had no name but care
      and in the fluid's flood
of cleaning and tucking in
what chance did I have
but lifting a soup spoon to your lips
the flavors of our final connections.

5

To breath in memories of sin
and in the fluid's flood
    to mark down passages in time
but yet to find the beauty in the sinister
of what has befallen
after hours and days passing in notice
so that our time together
    be fresh as roses in blossom
even as those flowers wilt away
hopelessly
and time becomes a measure of dessication
here where I am standing and you are sitting
leaning your head against my hip
as we contemplate nothing.

6

Our house close to the rambling of the sea
that seems constant witness
    of what has befallen
yet beckons us to the self's exit into a clarity
down wind from transpired
difficulties
and you my love were harbinger
    of what I would be following
so that our time together
in those last days
became eternal in a present moment
that remains still in memory
as if a photograph in constant motion
empty of tears shuddering and regrets.

7

As the literal was transcribed
and the story arrived at midpoint
    we found ourselves in a new city
pining for those earlier days
in which what's left behind is prelude
that remains still in memory
of all those figures haunting us
until in darkness and this city's lights
    were harbingers
of what I would be following
into these calm adventures
just the two of us
and dare I speak of loving you
which is inadequate.

8

Things that were there are no longer there
as when in the old kitchen
    I wonder why I'm here
until in darkness and this city's lights
all becomes apparent
in your recipes and utensils
    your hands in the rubber gloves
which is inadequate
and is not you
your mind and shoulders and your smile
in thoughts of you coming unbidden
without any effort
so that here you are not in thought but in vision
and here I am the lonely boy.

9

I wonder why I'm here
    after rage in your sickness
sitting in this whicker chair
a purchase agreed upon
well before construction of this interior
house world done
    without any effort
so that gatherings of objects might define
a marriage in eclecticism and did
even as water on oil
and after these endings that left all beginnings
two became one
as in darkness before lamps were lit
to reveal these empty spaces.

10

My days now in oblivion
of useless meandering in the leavings
    even as water on oil
allows no emulsion
and the now is only embarrassment
as in darkness before lamps were lit
    to reveal the shadow of your smile
to the sides of faces engaged in conversations
I take little part in
    telling jokes that are a mask
and when the party is over and your face
has faded for a while
I take momentary pleasures while cleaning up
until your face appears again and I am lost.

11

When you showed me the photographs
taken when you were younger
I remarked on your beauty
    though beauty is in the eye of the beholder
and I don't believe that
since I saw your spirit in you as something
I take little part in
believing in your autonomy even when the past
has faded for a while
though in the clutch of self pity
    that is my nature these days
who once was no more than a late adolescent
shrugging into your presence
full of frustrated desire.

12

The mind in a caravan of lost opportunities
that is my nature these days
even as I try to catch up to your ashes
    and scatter my own above you
in a time slowly approaching
and I don't believe that
heavenly choirs will attend us
    even as relatives morn
until they too join us
and time stops
though in the meantime let me go on
even in this oblivion
    where angels parade in old paintings
and words ride into a void.

13

In a time slowly approaching
where memory ends
      and your favorite music
is defiled in the ears of the living
though you would give it kindly and with a smile
I can still see
      even in this oblivion
where days are counted toward an ending
that will gain us nothing
since your spark of life has been extinguished
leaving this other half
      to stand beside the sedum
given to you by our cleaning lady
called live forever.

14

As conversation rots in the mouth
unaccounted for at sunset's prelude
of passions last meal
      while winter fell in crystal snow
and time becomes a measure of dessication
yet beckons us to the self's exit into a clarity
      until in darkness and this city's lights
so that here you are not in thought but in vision
well before construction of this interior
and the now is only embarrassment
though in the clutch of self pity
      that is my nature these days
since your spark of life has been extinguished
and I can only say goodbye.

## That Way

The kids, my love, are drawing circles in the sand.
How simple their devices,
a stick, laughter, some imagination.
     These certain children are just.
Their circles are not.

No sand in the inland summer,
so jumping games,
something we didn't get around to,
though at times, in your presence,
I might have jumped for joy.

You are gone.
The circles have given in to the tide.
The children are gone.
There's a dear woman beside me.
She doesn't know what I'm thinking:

     summer on Bonaire.
The fruit boat in from Venezuela.
You are delighted.
That night, in our dark hut,
iguanas scratched on the tin roof.

How foolish to consider
these foolish things:
     your wedding dress in the closet,
still, after forty-nine years. A hat and a scarf,
a favored coat.
I could see you in them, wearing them all.

Yet I am not alone in my madness.
Memory: there you are
      in my silly construction,
a wooden hand and a foot,
the way, in illness, you cared for me
hand and foot.

And just walking down the street together,
side by side, not holding hands,
your awareness
of everything: fabrics, buildings and blown leaves,
      all the way to the earth's rotation.
And where you stood was center

            and gravity. What chance did I have?
One evening in darkness: your hair,
      the tilt of your head, that little light.
You are reading, and from my vantage
you are viewed only in silhouette.

These impossible images, fixed on film
      in some kind of photography
and quite dead.
Let me listen to your music,
keep you alive
that way.

On a forthright spring afternoon,
surrounded by the wonder of her flowers,
and still stunned,
it came to me:
      I had not thought of you
in two long days.

## The Meal

Something out of the corner of the eye
or in the eye;
      something discovered in passing
[not nous in the  passage]
within time spent in the concrete [a ladle,
a knife], recipes
fallen down from a bookcase.

The meal of the day is flanken:
      [Put meat in. And cover with water
or a little more than cover.]
blessings on the animal's flesh treated
so well in the preparation.
          And carrots in the corner of the eye
in time spent in the passage. And dumplings
formed carefully in the hands.
[Cook until meat
falls from bones. Constant skimming.]

And of course time passes in the treating
      [turnips in the corner of the eye
ripening]; remains of the animal passes
to a final destination
        [location possibly noted
in new growth], and we have come through
yet again.
      [Put carrots and dumplings in. Continue
until all is ready.]

Something in the corner of knowledge
      [in the nose in the passage],
which is not knowledge
[in the great passage] formed

carefully in the hands, but flesh of the animal
treated to carrots and destination
    [the only passage], through yet again
to rise up in the new growth
in the garden [eggplant,
        basil and broccoli],
something out of the corner of the eye,
received in the eye
[the nose].

Blood of the passage in constant skimming
which is not nous but coming through
    yet again partially changed
until all is ready. Something [a side dish,
wine, a ladle] in a corner in living,
a woman's knife and dumplings.


The meal of the days is discovered
    in the corner of the eye's passage,
in the flesh heated to release scent
        of garlic for the nose
[in the corner where a woman stands],
    for the palm cupping the ear
to the bubble
[until the meat falls]
which is not skimming knowledge.

Fallen down from a bookcase,
    ingredients of the careful lesson
[a recipe, a code, a knife]
gathered up from the floor of the dead
    [location possibly noted]
given back into the corner of the eye,
not nous in the passage.

Seltzer on the table, a ladle, elbows,
compliments to the chef
    [into a fanfare], treated
to carrots and destination.

And of course time passes
    in time spent in the passage,
a simmer in the corner of the eye fallen
down from a counter,
recipes from a bookcase
there on the floor of the dead.
        Flesh of the beast as a burnt patient
the woman is carefully nursing,
    down in the scent of garlic,
anticipated skimming,
putting the meat in [casual sacrament]
out of the corner of the eye, caught
    partially changed
in the great passage [the only passage].
Cook until meat falls from bones,
until carrots grow vibrantly
dark orange color
    in time spent in the concrete
[wound that will not heal].

Yet again in the conversation
      [location possibly noted]
of new growth in the corner of the eye,
sacrament of the animal's passage
    within skimming of destinations
[garlic, a ladle, a knife],
fanfare of compliments
for the chef's knowledge [but not nous]
of blood breathing
in the nose in the passage

[desire for reversal of fortune]
	in the nose in the passage
of blood breathing
for the chef's knowledge [but not fallen]
	fanfare of compliments
[up from the floor of the dead]
within skimming for destinations,
	sacrament of the animal's passage
of new growth
in the corner of the eye
in a garden of eggplant and tomato
	[location possibly noted]
yet again in the conversation;
the meat falls down from the bones,
carrots grow vibrantly
dark orange color
	[the wound that will not heal]
in time spent in the concrete.

Out of the corner of the eye caught
putting the meat in [casual sacrament],
in the great passage
	the woman is carefully nursing
flesh of the beast as a burnt patient
there on the floor of the dead
recipe  from a bookcase,
a ladle in the corner of the ear fallen
	in time spent in the passage,
[the meal of the day is discovered]
and of course time passes
until all is ready.

[Flanken. Carrots and dumplings.
	Blessings on the animal's flesh
treated so well in the preparation

                and on the woman's hands in the corner,
a sacrament
fallen down among recipes from a bookcase,
the floor of the dead littered
        in the great passage] The only passage.
[Ingredients of the careful lesson,
a conversation
        in the concrete, which is not knowledge.

Blood of the passage in constant skimming
of the meat put into a simmer
on the passage through
        to a final destination,
location possibly noted
in new growth.] And we have come
into the corner of the eye yet again,
partially changed.
Desire for reversal of passage
up from the corner of the eye's recipe
[casual sacrament],
        not fallen discovery. The floor of the dead
grows vibrant, garlic, a knife, a ladle,
                ingredients of the conversation,
a fanfare: careful lesson [location
possibly noted] in new growth.

    And we have come through yet again.
Flanken. Seltzer on the table, elbows, a woman
brushing the floor of the skimming.
        Off in a corner of the eye,
a bouquet of carnations, a pot, a ladle;
the wine blood is breathing.
        It's getting late; time passes.
Let us begin the meal.

# SEE / SAW

## Bird

Who can name the flavor of the bird's death?
In generations she has passed along her song.
The answer is hidden in the nest.

Awkwardly have we been singing all along.
The bird might have sung a different tune.
Who can name the flavor of the bird's death?

In winter and summer and even in June
her sad serenade toppled even the choirs.
The answer is hidden in the nest.

The ones who speak of nature's ways and plans
head the list of all meticulous defiers.
But who can name the flavor of the bird's death?

We can. The women can. The poets can.
All explanations are adamant about the outliers.
The answer is hidden in the nest.

We see her as a history of girls.
We gaze upon the magic in her feathers.
But enough of our melodramatic musings.
Who can name the flavor of the bird's death?
The answer is hidden in the nest.

# See-Saw

Scandalous is the moment
felt by the children
whose long board rests
    upon cinder blocks
in the back yard
he on one end down
and she in the air
    braids bouncing
as the sun gives up the ghost
and these children
like all others in yards
and streets all fall down
then rise back up
into the future.


2

As the sun gives up the ghost
these beautiful children
as least in the eyes of parents
fracture the silence
    under birds singing
unconcerned as night comes on
and parents are calling "come in"
    "come in" while those others
weep for the past
and she in the air
throws up her arms trusting
the other that we learn
not to lift us up
even as we dance.

3

And later do these movements
come upon them
these beautiful children who are no
    longer that
but cook now in undirected passions
for some other for freedom to
    fracture the silence
for tenderness and not mercy
for romance
but structure waits in the wings
and the games will soon be ending even
as they live
without any idea of future
as birds sing perhaps mocking them.


4

For now does supposed maturity
reside in them
even as they live
    these hours and days
up and down see-sawing for
romance
corning and going
    no ending in sight
for he who is always waiting
for the one to appreciate
all that he has to offer
    which is beauty he thinks
were he that sister
borne up and rising.

5

"I am the one
come up and rising
beyond maturity
     and yet alone
still wishing who is
coming and going
     in search of recovery
from days spent
in empty passion's painful
losses even as I go back down
     to find a woman
worthy of this perfected ego
that sustains me
as I see-saw days away."


6

"'Worthy of this perfected ego'
is the dance in which
my brother turns
     awkwardly while wishing
and yet alone
with memories
of a time when he was rising
     only to come back down
again earth bound
which should have been
the message in the dance
     while I held children
and a family
wishing for nothing more."

7

But then the world beyond
their simple enclave
rose up in arrogance
      only to come back down
in fire war and flooded shores
while crazy see-saws tumble
      again earth bound
and that which promised life
and limb denied it
so that some among
      the supposed safe
became refugees
and she was shaken by it
while he fussed with his hair.


8

A river flowed
rose up in arrogance
carrying garbage to the sea
      a supposed cleansing
of all disregard
and the children of children
      fish in the stream
catching what will not be eaten
even as the sister believes
her brother's lacks
      will dampen
and approach maturity
even at thirty
while crazy see-saws tumble.

9

"So let her ridiculous children
fish in the stream
      even as this uncle
comes to foretell a sadness
without such encumbrance
as days turn into years
      of monstrous successes
catching what will not be eaten
and love is an answer
      no longer possible
while closed doors hide
an expected outcome
in which the see-saw rises
into my future."


10

Death comes to haunt
of a child lost in the stream
      while closed doors hide
all grief in privacy
though a town can be the world
empty of see-saws
war torn
while rulers speak
      of monstrous successes
and at the town's borders
all loss is forgotten
and music continues
      dissonant in the flooding
of rivers headed for the sea.

11

The children are gone
and they in their sixties
    empty of see-saws
press on widow and one
completely alone
    all grief in privacy
turning to each other seldom
as if fate's hammer
where only for others
and they owned their days
    and years stumbling
while age brought on
supposed wisdom
in which comfort resided.


12

In their endings
caskets are lifted above
as if on a see-saw
    and children
no longer children weep
completely alone
turning to each other seldom
    wondering
what was the measure
of lives spent
his always in hiding
while hers rose up
in this same town
after all.

13

The song has ended
but the melody
lingers
over this small town
    as if on a see-saw
come to rest
where a river runs
    and lives spent wondering
what was the measure
of time as the rich progress
of a man and a woman
    forgotten
even as church bells laugh
and each ending is a beginning.


14 – Coda

As the sun gives up the ghost
unconcerned as night comes on
and later do these movements
    these hours and days
in search of recovery
awkwardly while wishing
and that which promised life
    while crazy see-saws tumble
catching what will not be eaten
death comes to haunt
and they owned their days
completely alone
and each ending is a beginning
of dissonant music.

## In Time

There was a woman I could not see
beyond the barricades, her face
in my mind.
Yesterday I saw her standing
      somewhere I don't remember,
but she is always there, in my dreams.
Is she my mother,
somebody else's mother,
      a forgotten girl?
The earth might crack open,
all of us rise up into the sky,
and yet I am still dreaming, mother,
of our tortured past,
still missing you.

Here, then, is the father of my imaginings,
tall, graceful, and lean,
yet not the one remembered,
      poor father, who in time
could no longer
stand or walk out into the sun.
How much wishing would it take
to alter the past,
to bring him forth healthy,
even in memory?
Is there nothing but an aged spirit
      here to do the dreaming?
There could be a boy in the park,
running to his father.

Almost as old as my mother
in my mind,
yet she is always there

   in dreams, forgotten girl?
Then think of our tortured past,
the three of us rising up into the sky.
Was she somebody
else's mother, children by another?
   Yesterday I saw her standing,
daydreaming beyond the barricades.
She was not there
   but somewhere I didn't know
or remember.
and yet I am still missing her.

Poor father,
yet not the one remembered
   when running to my father
who was standing or walking
graceful and lean then
and even in my imaginings
to bring him forth healthy.
   But I was a small child
in a man's mind bent
on altering the past.
Here then are my fathers,
both of them.
Still, in time, in the memory,
one father replaces the other.

My father was pulling the covers
from my mother's body in jest
   and I was crying mistaking
fun for brutality.
I remember little else of intercourse
between them,
no touch, or kiss,
   no loving fondling.

How foolish is the poetry
designed to capture the past.
      Add the atmospheric music,
then set the stage.
My mother in my father's arms,
holding each other.

Let down your hair.
Your beauty was contagious
      mother in frustration.
As all your plans were thwarted
endeavors on the way to freedom,
all of it, and you, gone now.
      How deep you're breathing,
taking in the sinister disasters
befallen husband and son.
      How long must I grieve mother,
even into my own passing?
We traveled through towns in a circle.
I too was burdened by a husband, father.
Let it now end.

# Four Dogs

## Max

I loved to be scratched
      on the back of my neck
as well as under my snout
and at the base of my tail
wiggling.

They took care of me,
let me roam in the country.

And in the city
doing my business in the park,
there were others,
little and big and mostly friendly.

Then in the apartment, warm and cosy,
they provided me with a place to sleep,
that soothing rug.
And dinner was always the very best.

I would walk between and beside them,
nuzzle their fingers with my nose.

I'm gone now.
I know they miss me.

## Dowager Dog

Ah, what the hell,
    okay, I'm fluffy,
can hardly see
with all this hair.

So she carries me,
all over,
all the time,

    but for gourmet eating,
a little roaming,
bumping into the furniture.

Her bosoms are soft and warm,
and I rest my head upon them
as we roam.

What a life!
She thinks I'm nice.


## The Coyote Pup

The coyote pup considers the young rabbit,
who hops by, brushing his nose,
Then maneuvers into the bushes.

The coyote pup is a baby,
and babies cling to their mother's calm wisdom.
The coyote pup's mother seems wise.

The coyote pup sees no essential difference
between rabbit and toad, his mother, foxes, and all others
who roam the earth in their curious, pleasurable, variety.

The coyotes have few predators.
They travel the woods, the golf courses, the cliffs.
Our coyote is not among them.

He's approaching the wolf's den,
smiling as the owner stares her rage upon him,
then charges and tears him to pieces.

When the coyote pup became a coyote,
then an old one,
his views hadn't changed.

It was his mother, after all.


## Little Dog (Yoshi's) Story

It's not nice to get an injection,
and it hurts: bah, bah, bah!

But Lois will protect me:
bow wow wow!

I'm happy as a clam
We're back home and I'm hungry.

bow wow!

Maybe it's time to chase my toys.

Maybe it's time to go out for business.
Maybe it's time to chew on the table's ankles!

I'm tired. I think I'll take a nap
right here in my mother's lap.

# Faith

The desire for meaning beyond
our paltry lives, our selves.
Meaning we can count on,
now or in the future.
      Love is not the answer,
and all these lovely flowers
and birds, even shelter
in the churches, is not enough.
The chalice is raised,
the alter boy I was
      falls to his knees,
and the congregation,
every single one,
believes in something unseen.

## Skeleton

1

Brother to a sled
but his bones desperate
    to turn and release
this human burden fragility
of his head beneath which
is the name called for
that echoes from the ground
that place
hidden as we hide all endings
and purposes while he glides
head forward perhaps mind first
into this turn
that may be the last one
foreshadowed.

2

Sinewless in the musical
dance of the calavera
    judge mother reporter
and he who fell down breaking
his clavicle unarticulated
as a child weeps for a bone
that is only the beginning
of that ending in which all might dance
hidden as we hide all endings
in our caskets wrapped in fine linen
or come to our rest in that fire
which echoes from the chambers
perpetual
and is the give.

3

Here at the shore's edge
    leavings of shark meals
as a child weeps for a bone
and seals moan
and behind me the fall trees
are becoming their skeletons
    yet even the children know
that is only the beginning
who are my lost children
though wished for in the silence
of this empty room
after a dinner of chicken
bones left behind on a flowered plate
while trees shudder skeletons in the night.


4

Though wished for in the silence
while trees shudder skeletons in the night
after pain in the tuberosity of the navicular
that will not heal
I limped to the casket of jewels
that were photographic mementos
lending credence to all losses
and therein discovered the daughter
I did not have
whose featured were those of some lover
forgotten
who may have been that mother
delivering the children of my imaginings
wet smiling placental and cord.

5

I stood among the tree skeletons
searching for morels
whose features were those of some lover
lost in the memory
and shriveled beyond recognition
    so that her brains come straight
to the pan scalded yet sentient
in my imaginings
lending credence to all losses
of those particulars
that have brought me this sadness
upon which I stand self-accused
now in this unconcerned night
forever burdened.


6

She lingered high up on the cliff
watching her children
play in the ocean's surf
lost in memory
of the one who might have been
of those particulars
that urged her eyes and brain
to those imagined lovers
    who were only empty
shadow figures
and these children
    a boy and a girl
built a sand castle
as if it were their home.

7

The bones of the fall trees
have no memories
of the one who might have been
present at the opening
as the breeze whispers through
their ribbed structures
up on the cliff as if they are
watching her children
at play in their building
of minarets and battlements
while the cage guarding her heart
shudders in those recollections
of a death discovered
in this beach town after storm.


8

Her painting was of that body
of a death discovered
      in bony nakedness
beside skeleton figures
that had been shark food
and in the painting were shadow figures
called up almost in memory
as the breeze whispers through
fall trees at cliff side after storm
and mothers in the painting are children
and children shall grow into mothers
but there is no father
to love her
not even in the painting.

9

I had made a pilgrimage
to the edge of sea
called up almost in memory
    where my children played
in surf and sand
beside small skeleton figures
who were calaveras dancing
on sand castle battlements attended to
    so that they did not see me
and the fires burning in pits
of sand holes holding lobster and corn
were only shadow figure
yet the children and mother
were mine even in death.


10

In memory of the scapula
the bruised rib
then late thoughts of the ischium
    and the pelvic girdle designed
to admit children
who were calaveras dancing
to the songs of these nether bones
and the craniums holding love
were only shadow figures
of days gone by
though the phalanges
reach up from the grave
still desiring
beach castles fires and a woman.

## 11

She stood at the edge of the cliff
watching her children
      and the shadow figure
still desiring
things that bore no touching
like skeletons in sand castles designed
to admit children
and it had taken time
in which he sat at the bedside
day and night until the ending
which was their beginning
      so bone touched her bone
of he who is now gone
though there on the beach watching.


## 12

At the opening
her paintings hung on walls
depicting the sand and sea
      in faint abstraction
of pigment colors
and the shadow figures
of children dancing
were calaveras
anticipating the arrival of the dead
as he left the opening
for the beach and
things that bore no touching
while she missed him
only briefly.

## 13

The figures in the surf through water
were his escaping children
a boy and a girl
      in vague abstraction
floating upward as he went down
anticipating the arrival of the dead
and his soon skeletal remains
as he swallowed sea and kelp
and the memories
of beach fires
lobster and corn and the woman
      wife mother lover and artist
who was not there
on the cliff watching.

## 14

This human burden fragility
sinewless in the musical
as a child weeps for a bone
lending credence to all losses
      so that her brains come straight
to some imagined lovers
while the cage guarding her heart
as the breeze whispers through
called up almost in memory
and the craniums holding love
which was their beginning
      were calaveras
on the cliff watching
and dancing in their bones.

## Trees

These massive pines have lost their needles
permanently, trunks now twisted in an agony
of thirst. They look like giant anacondas
sucking up what sustenance remains
to filter in through rotted bark.

Somewhere in them is the vague feel
of chipmunks, red squirrels,
the delicate touch of many birds.

When they were young I walked among them.
Then, in middle age, they swayed in comfort
in the breeze. Their skin when they were old
became pock marked and fragile,
very much like my own.

Now they are dead and yet still present,
their burial upon this earth I walk upon.
We hide the dead, but trees luxuriate
even after their passing. I walk among them.
I am not dead yet.

## Wind

Everything is up in the air.
Down wind in the lush meadow
she holds tight to her bonnet, her ribbons,
      and he fusses with his hair, watches
the table cloth, the napkins,
and the champagne cork
all blowing away
      into the shook loose blossoms
that fill the air, as snow might
later, in the relentless gusts.

The winds are often our enemy:
forest fires, cyclones, tornadoes,
      all fueled by winds,
those ill ones that blow no good.

I saw a Grosbeak at the feeder.
Her wings rose up to savor
the light warm breeze
      in those spaces
where the wind subsides for moments,
gathering its forces.

But what about the air
in which the bird's wings rise,
curtains and summer flies,
smoke rings?

Let's enjoy the breeze that lifts our clothing,
the wind in her hair, her underwear
fluttering on the line.

# Fire

I saw a horse set afire
on the crest of a cactus strewn hill
in Arizona, when I was a child.
     A dead horse, but she came alive
and danced in the flames.

Fire's heart is relentless.
     Everything gives in:
photographs; important papers;
that dress you once wore,
enjoying yourself for the first time;
your husband's easel,
and your grandmother's old country vase.
All of it gives in.

But of course there are camp fires,
     that cast iron stove in your
living room,
comfy, some fancy fire pit.

In the end there is only fire,
earth, and the other two.

And yet I can't dance in the flames,
though my time will come,
yours too.

     But while we are waiting,
let's enjoy the fire in our hearths,
let it warm our hands and knees.

# Rain

I'm in the house.
Rain beats on the windows
and on the deck,
turning blond wood amber,
      and beyond: oak, his foreign
sister ablaze in red,
a blanket of yellow wild flowers
(in the mind), skeletons of dead pines.
All soaked in rain.

Benign bullets pound the shingles.
It's flooding my watering cans,
      where even miniature boats
would flounder in the waves and sink.
And Tom
checking his flowers
in the rain,
wind stirring his bubbling slicker.

Rain gets to me.
(those old romantic memories of course).
Still, we wait for rain, needing it,
and when it comes it's annoying,
oh woe is me, but then
      we begin to feel we live in it,
nurtured. reinvigorated, thoroughly watered.

I hate the rain, I mean,
on the other hand,
I love it.

# The Sea

Once again the flavor of the sea
	comes in with the tide, the air,
the salt I taste with oysters
on my tongue.

In the west the rivers are sand,
	but the sea salt requires
that I drink, and savor.

I smell it in the trees,
in bird nests, in the memory of your hair,
in my ongoing collapses,

such as they are, unnoticed,
though the bell tolls.
	What right have I, who is he,
to slumber so peacefully,
then moan about things?

It is in fact He.

## Nature

Now that nature is really seldom seen,
it's music in that foreign tongue
      drowned out by politicians
and those whose faces are in phones
conversing with the seldom seen,
I spend my time with birds
and rabbits as I rake dead branches
      into a pile, even though
my hip is aching,
and I don't know what the future holds.

The future:
soon leaves with grow,
the Orioles will arrive again,
the heart will beat
temporarily, and the grass
will grow up out of the ground.

Nature doesn't give a damn.
Rodents take up residence
      in the White House lawn,
horses neigh
and birds drop their offerings
on the shoulders of those leaving
congressional meetings.

And still I rake
and feel my hip ache.

# The Fall

How much time Lois
do I have until summer ends
and this house falls
      into receivership
whereby dying grasses swoon
as other hearts take up residence
and the potted basil
grows limp
after careful tending
of thistle in those feeders
      I have not made
though we have watched
the Goldfinch guarding
his subtle mate.


2

And this house falls
as you Lois
      do not break faith
even in winter's somnolence
after careful tending
though city hearts ache
      for spring renewal
under these snow blankets
where is both loss and coming gain
      but for that last night
when we both held fast as if
one body could be made from two
and finally the sun
broke upon the blanket where we slept.

3

These city streets
are now in glimmer after plows
dug them out Lois
while up north two houses
welcomed rain
      and finally the sun
lit those worlds familiar
in memory
of past becoming future
when we both held fast as if
our losses were our gains
and the repair of a lawn mower
fixed our lives as well
as you climbed up on the seat.


4

Should this heart ache Lois
in stutter step
while old bones shift pain
to guts head and eyes
what is remembered
      remains vivid
somewhere
of past becoming future
that is no more than present
understanding since
our losses were are gains
as we might have been dancing
though sitting
in our chairs watching.

5

Do you remember moments
from your past Lois
while old bones shift pain
    that remains vivid
somewhere
in a town named for a fox
where the child that was you then
played in a house yard
where a woman had raised rats
    and you slept beside another
who was older wondering
about a future that did not exist
but for tomorrow and the day after
in a child's vision of discovery.


6

Dark dreams come upon us
as if seen through a dirty window
    that one Lois
in a town named for a fox
where bones danced in visions
as the flesh of one fell away
who was older wondering
would it be city or country
    or would it be that heaven
of deep distance relief
under wings that are no more than fancy
though the clock still ticks
in the present
promise of a future.

7

I have boiled lobster for dinner
while you have brought the salad
    and a tricky dog with a name
Yoshi Lois who
though the clock still ticks
can jump and lick and smile
until dinner and wine are done
and we are in the tub
    of deep distant relief
after which wet then dry
we 're in the bed reading and touching
then drifting away wondering
    would it be city or country
or could this be paradise.


8

The park was empty Lois
but for a woman walking
    a dog that strained at the leash
though quietly who can
jump and lick and smile
even at four a.m.
when the stores are shuttered
though the clock still ticks
and there is music in her mind
    and in her heart thankful
for a dog at home
in her arms
as the stores receive their deliveries
even as the sun rises.

9

Love is the answer
       to an old man's ills
and his spirit active
even as the body goes down
       into some oblivion
but for a woman walking a dog
even at four a.m.
and he is the one watching
at the window
though quietly who can
remember and forget everything
but Lois your coat
held tight against the wind
and your dog dancing.


10

And he is the one watching
this street of dream
       thinking of your fit body
which is elsewhere and yet here
on the couch
as he turns from the window
in some oblivion
to find you Lois napping
       book open in your lap
and once again the dog beside you
where I have been
no longer lost
in fears of a future
that is now beginning.

11

At times beyond this country road
the woodcock's snort
      no longer lost
as I have been with eyes
that cannot see
what once was clear as day
      without fears for the future
since there is vision in the mind
still nuanced
of that bird's beak
seen in photographic illustration
loved as you love them all
even the absent Mockingbird
Lois lover and friend.


12

And so I come close to the end
of poetry and the flowers
in your garden
soon burgeoning as spring arrives
loved as you love them all
in spite of the closing down of days
that cannot see
a future gorgeous as the present one
that linger in the mind's eye
Lois though no ending
is foreseen
and we'll be dancing
as our futures
dissolve into a common past.

## 13

As the dog barks for attention
in spite of the closing down of days
and you stand there
     holding the leash
while I wonder who is the master
as our futures
might depend upon one
who is demanding in his wishes
to be held tight Lois
all the time and every time
even in the bed between us
     who will soon be sleeping
then awaking to his licking saying
let's go out into the world.


## 14 – Coda

How much time Lois
even in winter's somnolence
when we both held fast as if
somewhere
while old bones shift pain
under wings that are no more than fancy
until dinner and wine are done
though the clock still ticks
even as the body goes down
and once again the dog beside you
as I have been with eyes
soon burgeoning as spring arrives
in spite of the closing down of days
that pass into our future.

# Standard-19:
## *I Live Dreaming (Vivo Sonhando)*

The window holds the secrets forgotten,
framed there,
    that which is common
to our passage beyond understanding.

Honeysuckle's blossoms
    fall away into dreaming
of times gone in oblivion.

I know
nothing of solitude,
    that place in which to rest
these weary bones, this weary mind,
perhaps an arbor, a chair.
I know nothing of them.

There was a basement cistern,
dark water fearfully
could not be touched by the child
I was then,
already a dreamer.
I don't believe that you're gone.

But now it's fall.
The foliage that's bearberry,
hog cranberry,
the shaking rage of the scrub oak
    in the window. In the soft wind
the juniper is still,
and the thin paper white birch beside it
is losing its life, its leaves.

Their fall is a feathered flood
through which is revealed
the skeleton,
      one turned leaf remaining
at the end of a dry limb.

She is dreaming up the remaining sustenance
in that last collapsing vein.
She sucks it out.
      There is only this
and then oblivion.
Banality of the many frequent deaths.

"Not so fast!"
There are tamales,
there is the fleshy gourd on the sill,
      there is vision
and all that the eyes, the touch,
the hearing, and the crazy dreaming
my whole life away
behold.

"Right."

And it's fall. The year has ended,
      if you count that way:
winter is a gracious host,
protector of the premature,
seeds frozen, waiting
for thaw, for spring,
in which the crops push up from the earth,
      green, yellow, red, "you name it."
All is coming to life, giving
until summer,
      and still there are fruits to be picked,

potatoes among them,
summer squash.

And so it's fall,
and I live dreaming, day dreaming
    that my life could return,
those parts I've been dreaming of,
that cistern,
blessed holidays,
music played by a trio in a tent.

This window holds the secrets forgotten.
The dump is not kind to the fallen,
be it casket or fire.

The dump,
that ironic "transfer station,"
    no documents required,
though dreaming you're hearing this song,
dreaming I'm holding you,
all of you, in memory.

Fall.
Understand me.
Understand my passage
beyond spring, my dreaming
of winter's approach,
which is only a dream in this rain.

Crazy
of a life still born in this present,
    which is never the present,
nor the future, but the past.

I've been dreaming of the sea beyond
this window, forgotten dancing,
a lump of coal. Then weeping,
then forgiving.
There's a train whistle in the distance.
Get beyond it.

"Okay."

Wishing and hoping
      and knowing it's wrong,
as is the dreaming, but for the looking:

      a dove perched on the feeder,
weeds that need pulling,
the mowing, cooking
and cleaning in minutes slowly passing.
This is today, right now.

Every time I've dreamed of you,
you've gone away,
      into this body's storehouse.
Let's keep it that way
and no longer dream about it.

## Winter in This City

The sparrows back up
into the breeze
eyeing those cast aside crumbs
that have fallen from the hands and mouths
of unconcerned humans. But
    what the heck,
what's going on
is the common winter dance
here in this city
where the landscape defies forest,
    and Christmas cards
depict buildings,
    and the people in them
are dressed for dancing
and not pumpkin picking, or searching
the woods, with guns, for turkeys.

To be happy in this neighborhood
in winter,
    happy in the bakery on the corner,
in the young women with babies,
laughing and playing
around the old, dignified, statue of the Goat,
    in the horns and traffic signals,
in Ben Franklin's invention of the busybodies,
that look down from high windows,
examining their stoops.

Then do mine eyes
fall upon the old lad
    seen through this window, her walker
struggling in slush,

frustration and anger in her thin arms.
      It could mean nothing.
We all get as old as I am,
who continues only
in poetry and sentimental journeys.

In some houses in the country,
the old sit and ponder in rockers,
      but here in the city
they move through the street,
gather in intelligent clusters
and speak of politics and what's for dinner.

But I started with sparrows,
      little guys that peck near the feet
of he who stands reading a map
in moments of sunlight.
There's his wife, rosy cheeked
beside him.

To have traveled a long distance
      (by their looks it's Norway),
backs to the bakery,
they seem puzzled.

Then a man in an overcoat
stops to help them.
      It's the way of things,
here in this city.

I have been often to the country,
where it is peaceful and good for meditation,
      and I stay there
and study birds and flowers. It's wonderful
to be there,

but soon enough the itch begins, too much peace,
    too many birds,
and here I am at this window.

The stop sign at the corner has a flashing red light,
but the cars rush through without care,
    except when people with dogs,
old folk, mother's pushing baby buggies
    step out at the crossing.
Then the cars all stop and wait,
often impatiently.

I'm impatient
for the country when I'm in the city,
and it's the same
    the other way around:
it's the trees, right, those rivers,
    and those glorious wild blueberries,
those damned blueberries!

So the voices echoing off the park's cement,
the colorful bodies, the intensity,
the energy.

Good Lord, here goes sentimentality yet again.

Okay. So that's the story, no more
    than a reflection about unsettledness
and city life.

# Mystery Stories

1

The story comes back to haunt you
in a manner of speaking
        where you're sitting
the jewels in your hand.

What did she say?
Don't worry?

        And I didn't.
The car would be out front
and waiting
        but it wasn't.

Sitting here in my cell
the jewels are not jewels
but worry beads.


2

Her body was soft
yet firm
and oiled from head to toe.
        He knelt over her and stroked her.
Then he squeezed her cheeks, very gently.
She looked up at him.
Was she gazing through him?
How old was she again,
fourteen?
        Delicious, he thought.
Then the door was breached and there was yelling:

"Pedophile! Child molester!"
They gathered at the bed side
      as he reached out for his robe.
Then they shook their heads and laughed
and headed for the door.
      He heard one of them:
"Can you imagine? A rubber mannequin,
a young one."


3

When the message
is imbedded
in the story
of it
there is nothing
but the story
and the strange
emanations
for the reader
who is the recipient
and half-crazy
in need
for discovery
of what the message means.


4

The darkness in the room was not total.
He could see the vague image of her face
in the oval mirror. Was she smiling?
What was she doing here?

He'd come down for a bottle of his best
in order to salve the wounds
in the gathering.
Since the murder they have been distraught.

The glimmer on the wine bottles,
nine o'clock.

An automatic light has come on,
and he can see the ghostly image of her body,
something in her hand.

Now she's moving around the workbench.
Neither of them speaks,
even as she's coming toward him,
almost floating in her dress-up garments.

He can't judge her intentions.
He's always loved her.


5

Did you see Mr. Castoff remove the letter opener from the table?
It's Kauzloff.
Did you see Mr. Kauzloff remove the letter opener from the table?
Yes, Sir.
Around eight o'clock, shortly after the murder?
Yes, Sir.
You don't seem to have much to say.
No, Sir.
And why is that?
It's your questions. They don't seem to ask for more.
You're questioning my questions?
No, Sir.

By, God! I'm going to get something out of you!
Hot under the collar?
Now you listen to me. Mr. Kauzloff is a very important figure. A Congressman
after all. And I'm gravely suspicious about your story.
I haven't told a story.
Your story is that you were in the parlor, where you had no
business being in the first place. You saw Mr. Castoff...
It's Kauzloff.
You saw Mr. Kauzloff step up to the side-table, reach out, and
remove the letter opener.
Yes and no.
Yes and no! Yes and no! What the hell does that mean?
It was the money. I needed it.
What money?
To say it was Kauzloff.
And who paid you this money?
It was someone you know.
Now you listen to me! Spit it out! Who was it?
I don't like to say.
You'll say, right now, or you'll go to jail!
Okay. It wasn't Kauzloff. It was your wife.
Oh, my! Never mind. Get back to your duties.


6

She held her pen in the corner of her mouth,
her papers scattered across the desk,
and spoke around it.

"It was July and like very hot.
That's why me and the girls went to the park,
like the fountains and foot pools, you know?

And I found the wallet.

Then Ken came into this.
He like chased me and caught me,
an undercover agent,
and the wallet was his.

So like Ken and me have been married
for fifteen years, we've got twin little girls
and a beautiful baby boy.

Oh, your like not hear about the wallet?
 You're here about the bonds
and the embezzlement?

I can explain that."

## The Names

The city broadcasts the names
of universities
      and hospitals he visits
on his way to a distant home
of darkness
below carving on the stone
that announces
his previous place
and all might be there as they
exist now in this mind
failing
as the sun sinks and will rise
again as the carved names
suggest the inevitable.


2

Dear pilgrims passing
who were Paul Robert Armand
David and George
as well as all the others
who cannot be named forgotten
      folk on this journey
on his way to a distant home
not wished for
though the body desires
as the sun sinks and will rise
      into named days
without vision to number
each fault and kindness
in lost poems and journals.

3

Time left on the journeys
to Paris Aarau
     Oyestranda and Milan
gone now
though the body desires
a returning wished for
as it tumbles down
into named days
     of Mondays in cafés watching
those on the way to work
who are not the foreigners
though he is
perched there for discovery
as the clocks tick toward Tuesday.

4

There are named towns
at the ocean's border
     perched there for discovery
of nature's encroachment
as dunes collapse
and houses slip into this sea
     after storms that are
a returning wished for
by seals and the black racer
if they were able to wish
though there heads are lifted
     watching destruction
of that civilization
in which they play no part.

5

Some live at the border
of no return
where the named sea birds
    watching destruction
flock and dive into waves
that hold riches
of that civilization
    we have no part in
yet we are wishing
for better climates and those loves
and sea birds dancing
as we all might dance fruitfully
into a desired future
even as the earth shakes.


6

Even as the earth shakes
and the Bobolink remains
    in danger of extinction
sparrows weather
these descending changes
where he sits on a rock
    and those loves
that all have names
leave these collapsed horizons
for that better place imagined
so that he might take his place
and fend off
    these hopeless feelings
presaging life's ending.

7

Who is the he mentioned
named Leonardo
    that map maker
of both stars and earth
and the children
playing on the surfaces of his mind
    no more than imagined
as he studies named countries
where the lines he'd drawn
are fracturing
    and he remembers angels
at the flat earth's corners
in old map's promises
of wholesome adventures.


8

Hurricane
and the houses closing
are fracturing
or burned to his ground in fires
on this gentle
    and frightened earth
and the children
still dance in their early innocence
    though there's no water
and fire flows from the faucets
as politicians jabber
    their mouths joking about endings
while the earth continually shakes
and what will be left is promised.

9

On the bright side
there are houses standing
and a multitude of people seen
    through a winter window
on this gentle
snow filled yard
    beyond which other houses
and people who
still dance in their early innocence
though there are others
    that knew the score
yet this was Christmas
those few church bells
might as well smile and join in.


10

That same man was lost
though he had a compass
    that reassuring device
that he could not read
but he could see however vaguely
and could thereby negotiate
furniture and people
but for the ones he wished
to encounter
    though there are others
yet this was Christmas
    and as the sun sank into night
the lit windows of houses
surrounded and calmed him.

**11**

Quartets of voices without instruments
neither classical nor jazz
and yet they could hear them
      multiplying in the acid rain
that rumbled in this chamber
where some might believe
this was safety
      even knowing better since
all hell was breaking through windows
and some politicians were leaving
without regretting their actions
      in this end of days
as if they were only dreaming
in a nightmare of their own making.


**12**

Once again the names
are carved in the silent stones
and those left behind
      multiplying in the acid rain
are no longer deniers
of the poisoned world
moving toward coming extinction
in this end of days
after which there may be
a few birds singing
      who are no longer named
their songs no longer regarded
even as he looks out his broken windows
to discover what is not there.

13

Finally it is he
who is regarding
        the stones carving
and those left behind
of which he is
the reluctant messenger
of the poisoned world
in language that is not heeded
as smoke obscures
        stars and moon
and leaves that will not return
blow away in these winds
even as they carve more names
in these silent stones.


14

The city broadcasts the names
without vision to number
time left on the journey
        and houses slip into this sea
where the named sea birds
leave these collapsed horizons
playing on the surface of his mind
and fire flows from the faucets
        beyond which other houses
furniture and people
that rumbled in this chamber
their songs no longer regarded
and those left behind
will be names carved into stone.

# Darkness

I see the Goldfinch at the feeder,
violently yellow,
tossing seeds.

She joins him, and thistle falls
      into that remembered curtain,
the one hung over my childhood window.

There are trees spied
through seed gossamer,

      and beyond them, because it's twilight,
the trees shimmer branches that hold fruit
and offer a dark message:
this is only the beginning.

Then come the dark silhouettes,
vague images, colors, numbers, people,
      the way they all seem still
and hung
upon the grey sky.

Fiddle with the keys.
Push the font size up.
Close my eyes.

      And above the screen in reality
and through the window past
the Hummingbird
in the lush green
and a mushroom passing as broccoli,
      is seventy-five years ago. I'm at home,
looking around

         at the colorful cartoon coverlet,
my narrow bed puffed up in sunlight
awaiting me,
         Andy Panda, sharp black and white,
on the flowered pillow,
the clothes in my little closet,
their rich variety of color,
         and the curtain that got me here,
each thread visible
in light at the window.

I open my eyes
to a vague reality.

But I saw it so clearly!
I am slowly going blind.

## January

Jan, are you wary of your beginnings,
as if there were disasters waiting?
Don't worry,
for under the year's early snow
crocus bulbs are sleeping,
and time will tell rivers
to crack open and flow again.
Give it a while, Jan.
Forget the politicians
and their wars.
Forget all petty arguments,
for you are the start of things,
the promisings
we've all been waiting for.

# Hummingbird
*—for Lois*

Said she could feel their wings' breeze
on her cheeks
      hand feeding.

Seldom do people hate them
in the human world at least.

Their business is nesting and eating,
but who can deny their pleasure
in that amazing flight?

Nothing is certain these days
but the Hummingbird.

      It's impossible not to romance them.
I can see them
a few feet from my study window.

They dance.

# Birds

"How long before
brother moon rises
for the last time over me"
    were uttered in the mind
sitting in a chair in the grass
while inside
the woman prepared
what might have been the last meal
thinking of an ambulance approaching
on an otherwise placid evening
    one on which he could hear
music drifting out to the lawn
where he always sat his heart
huffing in that dissonant rhythm.


2


Absent chambers in the chest
of the fallen and risen dictators
while inside
was another country devastated
hunger and passion driven
thinking of an ambulance approaching
while birds and bombs fell
from the sky
and disease was everywhere
even in the minds of the young
without uniforms
who measured their days in minutes
while the old fell away early
into the accepting ground.

3

He gathered his children around him
a boy and a girl
hearts beating in unison
while his skipped in counterpoint
and love now was a burden
    even in the minds of the young
who could lend no parts of themselves
hunger and passion driven
in their world without memory
    traded in later
for wisdom approaching
those end of days
    even as the father
gets ready alone to leave.


4

It breaks his heart to watch
    the birds he cannot name
though they be yellow and lustrous
and "be" might come from the past
but then he too is old
and fancies the birds flock
    hearts beating in unison
full of memories
but he must pause remembering
    his journeys to many places
and those more vivid in the mind
because his eyes fail him
while he thinks of things to be done
the dead brush the lawn mower.

5

The birds were nesting in the copse
and Angela
was waiting for her beau
the light hearted one
who knew her name
    even before he approached her
and at the prom almost tackled her
but seemed to suppress the urge
a gentle man for sure
and now as well
    even in this coming end
then moving forth to loneliness
ah but look at him
as here he comes.


6

The burdens of the heart
that is not the heart
but the mind's lost carelessness
    comes back to haunt
even in these birds
whose carefree flights
and those songs becoming sad
    tunes to echo his regrets
that all have as near the ending
only vaguely anticipated
until the clock ticks toward finality
while he sits again in the yard
heart beating awkwardly
forgotten when his children arrive.

7

The birds are Goldfinch
House Sparrow red Cardinal the
      Lazuli bunting Nuthatch
Bluejay and among others
the Starling who robs hidden nests
while he sits again in the yard
watching everything
      that moves vibrantly
as he once did
though now nothing seems possible
but looking through clouded eyes
while his heart beats out the message
that only in this bird playground
does singing continue.


8

And now the world beyond him
stutters into its uncertain future
as bombs fall
      even children fall
innocent in their lack
of understanding
anything but toys and parents
the quality of the spaces
for playing streets and yards
over which the unnamed birds fly
      assuming nothing
more than his daydreaming
of a cleansed future
in which he will play no part.

9

Angela awakens to the sound
of stertorous snoring
      that approaches suffocation
as there is no turning
on the pillow in his dreaming
but what about her about her
and the children
over which Starlings fly
      always searching
and what about life as a survivor
for she is the one left
behind joining multitudes possibly
still weeping
while the fools laugh and grin.


10

The churches are empty
as the politicians are empty
      and flatulently speaking
in borrowed phrases
expected by birds bewildered wives
and their fellow gentlemen
yet still do they sleep
      as all of us do
without nightmare
ever counting votes like sheep
in their slumbers untainted
      by anything close to wisdom
and yet does the clock continue
to click time falling away.

**11**

They are dreaming as the past
becomes the present
    that can only be present
in the mind expectant of disaster
at home in this bed
in the world even these birds
flight always there and remembered
    vivid as is this past
of assumed wholesomeness
where they both were approaching sleep
remembering rivers picnics sudden showers
    in a time of no politicians
empty of all sadness and grief
that will arrive soon enough.


**12**

He put away his tools
financial records and medicine
    no longer needed
pay stubs glasses and certain books
and then he cut the grass
    and after that
sat in his chair in the yard
Angela beside him
leaning against his shoulder
    whispering into his ear
that there is still time still time
though there is little time
as the yard glimmers at dusk
before the sun goes down.

## 13

Let us not weep away
avarice the rights of women
     war and the pestilence
imposed on a nature once young
even as we think of passage
to those times that never were
although lived by as he wakes
     from sleep in the yard again
prescient now too late
dreams fractured
     all music dissonant
as words fail the heart
and only these birds feeding
are without guile.

## 14

On an otherwise placid evening
while birds and bombs fell
he gathered his children around him
and fancies the birds flock
and now too
the burdens of the heart
     Lazuli bunting Nuthatch
innocent in their lack
while the fools laugh and grin
without nightmare
empty of all sadness and grief
whispering in his ear
     as words fail the heart
even as he goes down.

## No Love Dying

"There will be no love that's dying here for me."
—Gregory Porter

Though in your last days you did not know me,
evidenced when,
      in the sad company of friends,
you asked, "Who *is* this man?"
I will not let it be.
There will be no love that's dying here for me.

But for your dusty shoes still in the closet,
a tool found in dirt at the path's side,
      but for your dancing, seated,
to quiet *Corcovado,* which is memory and not
cruel evidence, but for time's passage in pudding
and green spotted cheese,
but for that emptiness in the bed beside me,
      as if some silent eulogy,
I won't let it be.
There will be no love that's dying here for me.

A sweet old lady sold me flowers for my Asian vase.
This isn't true. It was you. Twelve leggy coreopsis,
      parchment for months now.
The death of love is everywhere,
in the beautiful Finch stunned by the clear glass,
      his fading yellow,
in the mirror, fallen from the rusty nail
and the afterimage,
      my face that empty outline
on the framed white wall.
Still

I will not let it be.
There will be no love that's dying here for me.

Embarrassing words hardly meant for poetry:
angel hair pasta
you boiled perfectly for me, memory.
Miriam in the singing of old union songs imperfectly,
your finger pointing when I reached again
for the bourbon,
in sleeping on mattresses under the stars,
    these stupid little things I loved you for
and still do.
I cannot let it be. The moon is full these recent nights,
gets blue. I'm getting sentimental over you.

There will be no love that's dying here for me.
Your chair moved awkwardly to the sunny window.

# Acknowledgements

The fourteen poems of 'My Little Plane' were originally composed to accompany a series of aerial photographs made by the artist Diane Burko. In that context, the poems were printed below the title *The Shadow Under the Shadow*. 'Reversal of Fortunes' was published in the Pip Gertrude Stein Awards For Innovative Poetry in English 2005–2006 (edited by Douglas Messerli, Green Integer, Los Angeles / Copenhagen, 2007).

Some of these poems appeared in the following magazines, to which grateful acknowledgment is made is made: *Anima, Atlantic Review, Boundary 2, Conjunctions, The Friendly Local Press, Gegenshein Quarterly, Mulch, New Directions in Prose and Poetry, New Letters, Ninth Decade, #, Occurrence, The Paris Review, Temblor, American Poetry Review, Boulevard, CrossConnect, The Colorado Review, Denver Quarterly, Downtown Brooklyn, First Intensity, Oasis, One Trick Pony, Golden Handcuffs, Mulberry Anthology, New America Writing, Dispatches From The Poetry Wars, Fiction International,* and *The Anthology of World Poetry of the 21st Century,* Vol. 10.

www.ingramcontent.com/pod-product-compliance
Lightning Source LLC
Chambersburg PA
CBHW021148230426
43667CB00006B/297